For Tom - Merry Christmas, and enjoy the open spaces!

SILHOUETTE ON A WIDE LAND

Alan S. Kesselheim

SILHOUETTE ON A WIDE LAND

Alan S. Kesselheim

Fulcrum Publishing
Golden, Colorado

The events, people, and places written about here are all based on real and true experience. The names of characters, however, are fictitious. The Steiger ranch and the Triangle brand are also creations.

Library of Congress Cataloging-in-Publication Data
Kesselheim, Alan S.
       Silhouette on a wide land / Alan S. Kesselheim.
            p.   cm.
       ISBN 1-55591-092-0
       1. Ranch life—Colorado. 2. Colorado—Social life
and customs. 3. Kesselheim, Alan S. 4. Landscape—Colorado.
I. Title.
F781.3.K47 1992
978.8—dc20   92-53039
                                                      CIP

Cover design and original illustration
by Paulette Livers Lambert

Interior illustration by Heidi L. Herndon

Printed in the United States of America

0 9 8 7 6 5 4 3 2 1

Fulcrum Publishing
350 Indiana Street, Suite 350
Golden, Colorado 80401

To Marilyn Grant,
who, more than anyone,
helped make this a book

Contents

Silhouette on a Wide Land

Introduction

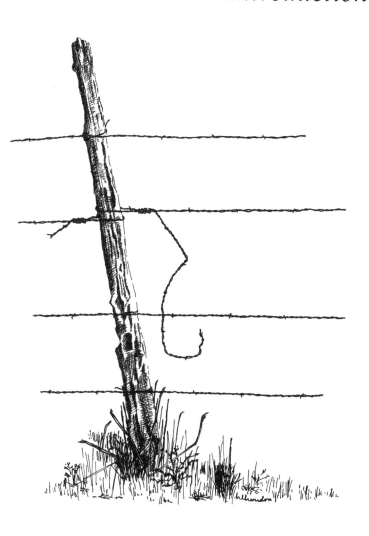

Introduction

I can't rationally explain, the way I can other segments of my past, how I came to spend a year of my life on the plains of eastern Colorado. Nothing in my upbringing or education pointed me in that direction. When I look back on that time, it appears as an unaccountable wobble in my life's orbit. I see it in the same light as I might view a stint in the military or Peace Corps duty in Honduras, a chunk so distinct that I might have it surgically removed to examine its shape and contours; a piece of personal history so unique I have to remind myself that I own it.

Because that year had such striking character, I remember it with an odd clarity, as if my memory bypasses the intervening years and connects directly. The dusty smell of ranch truck cabs, the way horned larks flurry from in front of a vehicle, the rough feel of a wooden fence post, the weight of summer heat on my neck. Years later, on some unrelated errand, I'm arrested by the memory of a swirl of pronghorn sprinting across the range, a memory with crisp edges and the power to stop me in midstride.

For most of my life I have been intent on objectives, on a track, unwilling to consider, or even see, the possibilities that glimmer briefly off down spur lines. The short-term truck-driving job that began my ranch experience offered itself at a point when I had lost momentum. Having graduated from college, dabbled in a few jobs and some travel, I felt spiritually lethargic, adrift, open to adventure.

I had little to risk by taking the job and the next month's rent to gain. The brief diversion had the lure of idiosyncrasy, a good story, something to do while I gathered myself again. But, once there, something like quicksand kept pulling me further in.

Weeks and then months went by. From truck driving I moved into farming and ranching, occupations for which I had no training and little natural aptitude. The closest I came to having a connection with that work was through my grandfather—a man I hardly knew at all—who had done some ranching in Montana. At numerous points I battled frustration and restlessness, thought about quitting. What am I doing, I'd wonder.

Although I had completed college, I embarked on an informal and challenging curriculum. I stumbled through lessons in rural living, ranch work, and often played the part of slow student. Because I traveled unfamiliar terrain, I tended to be alert, on guard, wary of ambush. I learned about myself.

Yet the longer I stayed, the more I became strangely attached. I spent most of my time alone. I was an outsider, by both inclination and circumstance. The few people I did come to know gave me some appreciation for the qualities of endurance, resilience, and humor that are required to cope with agricultural life on the High Plains. But my most significant human relationship was with two settlers who were never more than figments of my imagination, two people who never had names or more than a faint basis in reality.

I came to realize how little time has passed since the early, pioneering days of settlement. Only two generations ago people were risking everything to stake homesteads in eastern Colorado, grubbing out harsh existences, or starving, or fleeing from the unforgiving climate. The dugouts and shacks and one-room schools are still there. Men and women alive today remember those times. I was forced to adjust my generally ignorant view of the people who have inherited the legacy of frontier existence.

The proximity of those tough and dubious years makes our present domination of the land all the more incredible. In a matter of a few decades we have fenced and grazed and plowed and altered the plains so dramatically that early explorers and first settlers would hardly recognize them. We have also wreaked tremendous damage. Not just with the dust bowl. Not just against the buffalo and Native Americans. We have stripped away the protective vegetative cover, the very clothing of the plains. We have run off, sucked up, and diverted much of the life-sustaining water. We have eradicated all but a tiny vestige of the wildlife that once filled the broad vistas.

At a superficial glance our domination seems complete, irrefutable. But as time passed, I began to appreciate just how tenuous that control is, how exposed to natural forces we remain. When hot summer winds raised thick clouds of plowed topsoil or a spring blizzard killed cattle by the hundreds, that feeling of immunity, that buffering sense of security created by houses and machinery and technology quickly evaporated.

Since I was much alone, I noticed and observed the wildlife, even sought its company. The animals that exist on the plains now are the harried remnants of what once must have been one of the most awesome displays on earth. Less than a century ago wolves howled in the night and fed on herds of wild game. Grizzly bear, mountain lion, and elk lived in abundance and synchrony. No more. But the wildlife is still worth knowing, worth watching, furtive and anemic and despoiled though it is, for the mute beauty and astuteness it represents. It was in that unscientific study, that observation, that I most often found refreshment and serenity.

The environment, despite our industrious attempts to thwart it, calls the shots. The forces of wind and storm, heat and cold, that interact on the High Plains are pervasive and powerful, forces we ignore at our peril. The vegetation, the wildlife, the crops and livestock, even the humans, have no choice but to respond, to adapt, to pay heed.

That, more than anything, explains why I spent a year there. I began to come to life, to quicken to the pulse of my surroundings. Power like that of the plains either attracts or repels; you fall for it or you loathe it. The space, the wind, the

Introduction

---

exposure, the play of light, the dryness—bounty and bitterness in the same offering. Grudgingly at first, at times with fear and a kind of stubborn resistance, I was gradually seduced and entranced.

I began the year with no expectations beyond minor and short-term financial gain, with no affinity for ranch life. Inexplicably, my involvement deepened, my attachment grew, time passed, I discovered things. Then, when it ended, I found that I had earned great wealth that had nothing to do with my still-meager bank account, a wealth granted by an austere and beleaguered landscape.

Change in Course

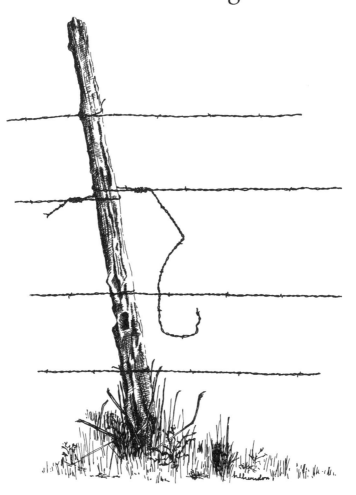

M eet me at Chicken Unlimited at one o'clock."
An inauspicious spot to interview for a job, I thought, pacing the sidewalk outside the fast-food joint. Norman Steiger already was fifteen minutes late. When I'd called the number on the microfilm at Job Service, he'd sounded like a man in a hurry, with preoccupations more weighty than deciding who would drive his ranch truck for a week or two.

Still, I expected more in the way of an interview than his brusque demand for a fast-food rendezvous. I assumed a more in-depth scrutiny of my qualifications would ensue when he arrived, that the location must somehow be conveniently located between his errands.

I thought about leaving. The truck-driving job sounded bogus. I resented being made to wait. I told myself that my need for money hadn't reached the desperate stage yet. Midday traffic on Tejon Street pulsed by in tight bunches. The sidewalk reflected uncomfortable summer heat. The smell of greasy fried chicken permeated the air. I alternated between sitting on a nearby bench and walking laps in front of the restaurant.

Norman showed up forty-five minutes late, whooshing to an abrupt, transmission-clicking stop in one of those city-style jeep vehicles—Bronco, Blazer, Wagoneer. He headed around the front grill at a late-for-a-bank-meeting tilt. I was surprised by his youth. Early thirties, I guessed. A short man, with a rounded, almost chubby face, wearing a western-cut sports coat, unscuffed cowboy boots. I detected a slight bulge in his lower lip—Copenhagen or Skoäl.

"Norm Steiger," he announced from several feet away, hand aimed for me.

"Al Kesselheim," I said, thinking, as our grip fell off, that the interview had begun.

"Can you start today?" Norm pushed his coattails back and rested hands on hips.

"Well," I shot a nervous look around, buying time, suddenly looking for a reason to decline, "I guess I'm ready."

"Good. Hop in." He started back for the driver's side.

For weeks I'd been looking for work, sweating over interviews for demeaning positions, responding to ads half a day late, not sure I wanted the job being offered in the first place, and here I sat, partially ingested by a deep bucket seat, riding through Colorado Springs with a new employer about whom I knew nothing but his name.

"I need you to pick up an irrigation motor in Denver." Norm flicked off the power switch to his car telephone and reached across me into the glove compartment for two slips of paper. "Here's the address. I think there's a city map in the truck."

I glanced at the second slip of paper. A straight pencil line marked Route 94 heading east from Colorado Springs to a circle marked Rush. Some distance past that, several right-angle turns without identifying signs broke off from the highway.

"That's the ranch where you take the motor. Find that gate." He pointed to an arrow on the crude map with his stubby finger. "Make sure you close it after you drive through. We'll meet you at the pivot about seven tonight."

Before I had a chance to ask what a pivot was, or to gather a salient point or two that might help, Norman swept the car into a large repair garage, flicked off the key, and jumped out. I followed around the rear end of a decrepit one-ton flatbed truck that I recognized somehow, with a sinking awareness, as the vehicle I was about to enter into partnership with.

A mechanic emerged from under the hood as we approached, and I had a brief glance at the engine. My main impression was of oil and grease. Pools of oil glistening in places I knew they shouldn't be, and caked, dirt-encrusted grease sheathing every cable, wire, and hose. Then the hood clanged shut and Norm strode off to tot up the bill.

I screeched open the driver's door and climbed into the musty cab. After dusting off the map of Denver that lay on the dash, I took a cursory look around the interior, enough to assure me that the abused appearance of the engine and body extended without any variation in quality throughout the vehicle.

By this time Norman had returned. "Got a map?" he called. "Okay, I guess that's about it."

He looked quickly over the truck and back to me with the confident gaze of an army commander who has prepared his men for every possible eventuality and has absolutely no equivocation about the success of the upcoming mission. "I left you a phone number if anything happens."

He started back out of the garage, leaving me still half in, half out of the truck, hand clenched around the smooth curve of the window frame.

"Oh yeah," he turned back, pulling a notebook from his breast pocket. "I need your Social Security number."

I gave it to him, sealing my commitment, but thinking all the while that I should have walked away from Chicken Unlimited when I had the chance. He turned again with a small wave, a dismissive gesture, heading for the next appointment, for which he was certainly an hour late.

"Jesus," I exhaled, sinking back on the grimy vinyl truck seat, hands on the worn steering wheel.

A busy mechanic pushed a button that sent the garage door clattering up and waved me out impatiently to make room for the next casualty. I turned the key. The engine groaned, sputtered, then roared to life. Billows of smoke and exhaust began filling the garage and I guessed, from the deafening racket, that the muffler had long ago been shaken loose on some dirt road. I lucked out by finding reverse on the first try with the floppy gear shift, about a yard to the right and down, and lurched backward out the door, looking up in time to see two mechanics vehemently waving away exhaust and dusting themselves off. ⎯

Change in Course

Within minutes I had bellowed onto I-25 north, coaxed the truck into high gear, and found my top speed at fifty-three miles an hour, although it was hard to read a speedometer needle that swung erratically across a twenty-five-mile span. Exhaust trailed behind me as though I were an interstate crop duster, and occasional backfiring truck farts loud as shotgun blasts punctuated my progress north.

August heat prompted me to try the air vent, but I was nearly blinded when a swirling tornado of dust, gravel, wheat seed, and engine dirt filled the cab. I slammed the vent shut. The open window would suffice.

I cocked my elbow out the maw of the window space and caught a glimpse of myself in the side mirror. In my rumpled and stained job-interview shirt, face specked with grit from the air vent experiment, driving a highway death trap to a mysterious industrial corner of Denver for a complete stranger I'd met less than an hour earlier, I made an unlikely picture. I rolled up my sleeves and grinned. The hot wind beating in my ears almost drowned out the noise I made thundering down the road.

What the hell, I thought, I could always quit. Norm seemed pretty unfazed by hiring a stranger without skills, character references, or appropriate background. One more laborer come and gone wouldn't mean a thing to him.

Rent on a small, dingy one-room apartment I'd taken in Manitou Springs would be due in a few weeks. My financial situation was strained. Months of traveling had consumed most of the savings from my last job as a teacher. I had been telling myself I needed something different, but besides knowing I wanted to live in the West, I had been vague about the particulars. Truck driving would buy me some time. I occupied myself by calculating the number of hours I needed to work at $4.50 an hour to pay my rent.

The sprawling southern spread of Denver brought me out of my musings. Through the polluted haze, the front range of the Rockies looked like a stage backdrop in need of repainting. I opened the cracked, coffee-stained map on the seat next to me, checked the address again, gripped the wobbly wheel with both hands, and girded myself for urban driving. Entering the city, I hunched toward the windshield and stayed in the far right lane, glancing at the map as I ticked off the exits, peering into the myriad corridors of industrial, commercial, and residential buildings. Cars whizzed by me as I roared along slowly.

The motor repair shop was relatively easy to find, once I'd wrestled the truck through a couple of tight alleys. In short order I had my cargo: a stocky, robotlike, bullet-shaped motor about four feet tall, winched onto the center of the truck bed and strapped firmly in place. Heading back south, I began warming to the occasion as I added up wages in my head. The exhaust-filled thunder I created along the way became more and more a familiar and enjoyable atmosphere.

I hit Colorado Springs going the right way at the tail end of rush hour, and felt my way toward Highway 94, going east. As I drove away from the city and the traffic-choked highways, I felt increasingly at ease. Only sporadic traffic, mostly pickup trucks, passed by. The rural two-lane road more accurately matched the vehicle I drove, and I grew more aware of my surroundings on the narrower, less over-whelming strip of asphalt.

The sun, visible in my rearview mirror, rode just above the massive, snow-packed ridges of Pikes Peak. Wafts of warm air clung to the bottoms of small, dry valleys. Highway 94 must have been set down with a ruler in the surveyor's office. It runs, with only a few minor jogs, abso-lutely straight east until it joins old U.S. 40 at Aroya. The small town of Rush lies thirty-five miles east of Colorado Springs, and vast empty chunks of land spread from the highway on either side, broken infrequently with straight, mostly dirt, ranch roads. My destination lay somewhere in the middle of one of those blank spots, somewhere southeast of Rush.

Crops I couldn't identify waved in the afternoon breeze or sparkled with water gushing over them from sprinklers. Corrugated metal sheds and older wooden barns grouped around large farm houses. Dirt driveways led into yards planted with islands of wind-breaking, shade-giving poplars and cottonwoods. Cattle grazed with slow methodical move-ments across the stubbly brown rangeland.

I noticed the town of Rush coming up and decided to stop at the gas station to fill the tank. After Denver and Colorado Springs, Rush looked like a ghost town. I waited at the pump until a large man wearing faded overalls shuffled out through the screen door. He looked closely at my city clothes, then at the truck, but said nothing as he fiddled with the gas nozzle. His freckled hands had knobby, arthritic-looking knuckles. On the way inside to pay, a broad circular thermometer caught my attention, eighty-four degrees. Moths beat stubbornly against the screens. The store seemed full of hovering dust, as if everyone who came in left a cloud of fine topsoil behind. The shelves were loaded with cans of chili, loaves of Wonder bread, packages of chips. I remembered that I hadn't eaten since breakfast. A calendar advertising an irrigation company hung behind the cash register—a bikini-clad model half reclining against a sprinkler. The big man made change and nodded curtly. Neither of us said a word.

A stolid one-story building that advertised itself as the Rush Cafe sat across the crossroads. Two or three ranch pickups were parked in front. I saw no people.

Every little side road that right-angled off the highway could have been my keyhole into the tricky maze of ranch country. Luckily, roads were few and most simply dead-ended in a field. Seven or eight miles east of Rush I downshifted with two evening-shattering retorts and took the first road of any consequence to the south.

Norman's sketch map proved remarkably accurate, given its paucity of detail. But then, there wasn't much to describe: two miles south, past one occupied and one abandoned home (the road bordered by three-strand barbed wire), then half a mile east and through a gate on a two-rut track.

It had been a while since I'd closed ranch gates. The truck rumbled and smoked behind me as I grappled with the gnarly post, finally squeezing the gate tight in an awkward bearhug, cheek rubbing against faintly aromatic wood. My shirt caught on a barb as I backed off.

The wheel track penetrated across a stubbly field and down a gradual slope to a concrete pad, where it suddenly ended. Nobody in sight. No Norman. No winch. Just Pikes Peak to the west and the High Plains sweeping to the twilight-darkened horizon in the east.

I shut off the engine. Evening silence and an impression of space washed in like a warm wave. I forgot about my unfinished errand and stood away from the truck, struck by the engulfing vastness of the plains. The contrast from the raucous truck cab I'd been encased in for the day was stunning. Night drifted toward me like a dry mist. The silence had a humming depth to it, and the late sunlight fired the wheat fields and range land to a deep blond burn. I breathed in the air like a drink, felt the heat exhaling from the exposed ground, and then remembered my predicament.

It was already after seven o'clock. A nearby rise afforded me a sweeping view. No movement. No people. Time passed, the plains cooled, my stomach grumbled. Twilight deepened like the quiet closing of a huge door. Could I trust Norman? Had he forgotten our arrangement? I picked stickers out of my socks while I waited.

Well after eight o'clock I heard an engine. Norman's boxy vehicle bounced across the field, followed by another ancient truck with a winch arm mounted on the bed.

"Find everything okay?" Norm bent carefully to miss his boots as he spat tobacco juice and motioned the winch truck back to the empty concrete pad. "Back up here," he gestured.

In five minutes we had the motor bolted down. Hardly a word passed. The other truck driver loaded his tools and drove away as soon as we finished, leaving the impression of a man who had been taken away from his supper.

"I have another motor that has to go to Denver tomorrow. Hit by lightning." Norm looked across the broad shallow valley toward a motionless windmill, momentarily losing his preoccupied air.

"Leave the truck here," he turned suddenly. "I'll give you a ride back to town and we'll come out in the morning to load up."

Norm hadn't closed the gate behind him but stopped so I could button up the fence for the night. He worked a ten-dollar bill out of his pants pocket to reimburse me for gas, then headed back to town at a steady seventy-five, talking briefly to his wife on the phone as nonchalantly as if he had been in his office.

"Lived here long?" he asked.

"No, I've been traveling. Just took an apartment in Manitou Springs."

"Gonna be here a while?"

"I'm not sure." I looked over at him. "I've been out of college for a bit. I don't really know what I'll be doing."

"Yeah, college doesn't seem like it helps much with that." He spat tobacco juice into a styrofoam cup.

"I can use the money till I decide what's next."

Norm grunted. "My family owns ranch land in Colorado and Kansas," he confided, by way of returning information. "Mostly it's land my grandfather picked up during the Depression."

The lights of Colorado Springs hove into view, a startling intensity after the miles of dark emptiness. Behind the lights the bulk of Pikes Peak loomed in the night sky.

"I run a water company, too." Norm's face was briefly illuminated by a street light. "Pump water from one of my ranches east of town and pipe it to the city."

The arid, treeless plains were vivid in my memory.

"There's more water than you'd ever believe out there, underground." As if he'd heard my thoughts. "Like a big underground river."

Embarrassed by the squalid place I lived in, I had Norm drop me off at the corner a block from my tiny apartment.

"You have a car?" Norman asked as I pulled myself free of the deep seat.

"Sure."

"Meet me out at the truck tomorrow, then. Ten o'clock."

Ranch Schooling

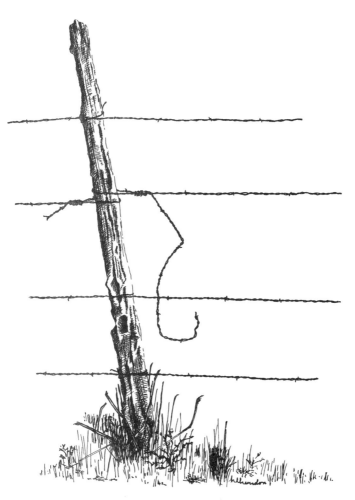

Ranch Schooling

For ten days or more the one-ton flatbed and I continued as a team. When I filled up with gas I'd routinely add a quart of oil, and leave it at that, assuming that any inquiry after engine maintenance would uncover more alarming problems than it would solve. I drove the vehicle in a state of ignorance, blithely trusting my luck—delivering and retrieving irrigation motors; picking up sacks of winter wheat seed, bundles of fence posts, bales of wire; acting as go-fer in the continual crisis management game that is the status quo of a ranch operation. I developed a guarded affinity for the beaten-up truck.

Norman never made it to a meeting with me less than half an hour late. I paced numerous Colorado Springs street corners, drank coffee at Dunkin' Donuts or McDonald's, even took to bringing reading material to while away the time. It's his nickel, I kept telling myself.

I rarely knew from one day to the next what my occupation would be. Part of me quietly resisted the disjointed work situation, the uncertain future, my lack of power, while at the same time I enjoyed the freedom that came with the absence of responsibility. Feebly resisting, I went with the flow.

Norm and I achieved, if not a friendship, at least a bantering ease with each other on our many drives together.

"One job I won't do for you," I told him one afternoon after an interminable wait at the John Deere dealership, "is be your chauffeur."

He chuckled at that, spat some tobacco juice. "I usually don't make bankers wait."

"Maybe I should lend you some money. Then you'd be on time once in a while!"

At the ranch I jumped erratically from one new job to the next, never sure if it would be my last duty. The few days of truck driving stretched into weeks of work.

Norman usually prefaced an upcoming challenge with, "Have you ever . . .?"

"Have you ever fixed fence before?"

"Nope."

"Can't learn any younger," he'd say, leading me to a tool shed, expounding on technique for three or four minutes, and rushing off again.

Driving the truck, loading and unloading cargo, waiting around for Norman had been easy duty. But moving on to actual ranch work made me nervous. New responsibilities expanded the horizon in ways I wasn't entirely comfortable with. And as I accepted Norm's instructions, I felt myself step farther into the hold of this unexpected entrapment.

Ranch work typically consumes long hours, is characterized by hard labor, and pays little. But fixing barbed-wire fence is in a class of torture by itself. Except for the efficiency and relative low cost of the stuff in a land blessed with essentially no natural fencing materials, barbed wire has nothing good to recommend it and everything evil to condemn it.

Ranch Schooling

If you're saddled with brittle, rust-coated spools of wire as I was, a victim of one of Norman's short-sighted austerity schemes, the demonic nature of the work becomes nearly intolerable.

Along with Steve, another hired hand, I spent a week at the task, replacing broken wire, tightening sagging legs of fence line, parceling off new areas destined for grazing or planting, all on the premise that Norm might want to buy and pasture cattle for the winter.

We rigged a primitive reel system by impaling a spool of barbed wire on an iron bar and setting it across the bed of the ranch pickup. As Steve idled slowly along a fence line, the wire spun off jerkily while I followed behind on foot, unsnarling rusty, sharp knots with my gloved hands.

Invariably, the old wire hung up on itself, broke, and had to be spliced back together. Invariably, when we stretched a strand with the come-along across several thousand feet of field, the final ratchet click would break it in another spot.

Gloves, jeans, and shirts became tattered casualties of the battle, and blood stained our slow trail of progress. August sun beat on us from above, frying-pan heat shimmered off the unshaded fields. Russian thistle stickers worked into our socks, ants boiled after us when we slammed into their homes with a posthole digger, making holes for the well-anchored corner sets. Sweat trickled and streamed down our faces as we sledge-hammered new metal posts into the baked and hardened earth.

On more than one morning I considered not showing up for work, putting an end to my ranch career. Norman still didn't know where I lived. I had no phone. He'd just call Job Service anyway. But each day ended with more fence strung and me wondering when I'd had my last tetanus shot as I cleaned my wounds.

I commuted daily from my apartment, stuttered across the breadth of Colorado Springs, and escaped out onto the shelf of plains. It took nearly half the driving time to extricate myself from the busy stop-and-start congestion of city. I realized with some surprise that I was anticipating the last stop light, the thinning traffic, the views of subdivisions replaced by sky and land, and a straight road arrowing into that space. My muscles and nerves relaxed with the opening vistas and empty road east of town. I developed my landmarks—the small towns of Ellicott, Yoder, and Rush, the few paved crossroads, the steep hill after Black Squirrel Creek, the mile marker I used to anticipate my turn toward the ranch. The fields that I now could identify as circles of wheat and alfalfa and maize flourished visibly as time passed.

On the way home, grimy and sweat-stained, my face and arms browner by the day, I more and more hated to leave, fought away the thought of my dark, cramped city dwelling. A bottle of cold beer between my thighs, I took in the wide wheat fields rivered by wind currents, and felt an upwelling exhilaration in response to the endless landscape.

— —

"Have you ever driven a tractor?" Norm asked one afternoon, as if he really thought I might have. "My damn driver quit yesterday!" He slapped a fence post angrily with his gloves. "C'mon, I'll take you around the field a few times. Gotta get the winter wheat planted."

The prospect of escaping the painful servitude to barbed wire brightened the future considerably, but Norm was taking a significant risk putting me behind the tractor wheel, and I wasn't at all sure I wanted the job. Driving a battered truck around the countryside or stumbling along with a spool of barbed wire was one thing; operating a John Deere 6030 tractor with a set of wheat drills behind was another.

But I followed Norm out into the field where the green tractor was parked and watched as he yanked himself up the small metal steps and into the glass-enclosed cab, motioning me in behind him.

"How much did this thing cost?" I called into his ear as the engine warmed.

"Thirty thousand, more or less." He fiddled with the dashboard knobs. "Close to fifty if you add in the drills."

I turned awkwardly in the cramped space to peer back at the triple harness of eight-foot bins hitched to the tractor, full of winter wheat seed waiting to drop into shallow furrows as soon as we set things in motion.

Norm flicked on an air-conditioning fan. The cab, especially with both of us crammed into it, was sweltering.

"There's your clutch," Norm demonstrated. "Here're the brakes, one right and one left. Be careful about hitting them unevenly."

"Bunch of gears here." He jockeyed the gear shift knob, and I looked at the bewildering diagram of forward and reverse speeds.

"Look, are you sure you want me to drive this?" I asked, knowing we'd already come too far to turn back.

"Easier than it looks." Norm brushed my anxiety aside. "Just drive around in circles all day. Nothing to it. You hardly ever need reverse." He slid the clutch to the floor and listened to the engine. "And I only use a couple of the forward gears for normal driving." He shoved the stick into a slot and eased off the clutch. With a jerk the tractor heaved forward, pulling its load of wheat seed, leaving behind us a neat set of parallel grooves. "See," Norm craned around to see everything in order, "it's so easy it's boring!"

We drove around the field twice, jouncing against each other, sweating despite the air conditioning, Norm holding forth in spurts about taking corners, stopping, checking the level of seed in the bins, instructions I clung to with a concentration equal to the level of my anxiety. Then he stopped—probably to escape from the crowded, overheated conditions in the cab—and called an end to the lesson. "It should take you a day or two to finish this field. Plenty of seed in the grain truck." He brushed off his pants. "When you need gas, go into Rush and fill up the tank in the back of the pickup. Charge it. Use the hand pump to put it into the tractor."

Abandoned again. This time with a fifty-thousand-dollar piece of machinery at my disposal. The fact that I could learn my way around the process with nobody watching provided little comfort. I gazed after Norm's car speeding away, towing a thin wake of dust.

The heavy tractor rumbled powerfully, a reminder of the task ahead. I stood in the unplowed portion of field, hands in my jeans pockets. It seemed that from the start the job had been a series of incremental steps of increased commitment, that quitting should have been as viable an option as continuing. I resented Norm's attitude, but if it really bothered me, why hadn't I walked away yet?

I fit my shoes to the narrow metal steps, opened the small door, and climbed into the cab. For a few minutes I sat on the heavily cushioned black seat and felt the throb of horsepower at my command, studied the gauges, gear shift, pedals, air vents, and turned to check the drills waiting as obediently as a team of metal horses. I gripped the wheel and let out a gust of breath.

After a time or two around the huge circle, I began to see what Norm meant when he said it might get boring. I labored completely alone under the hot blue dome of the summer sky, slowly beetling around an unrelievedly flat plane of dirt, frequently turning to eye the linear tracks that stretched behind, so as not to miss a swath. Once in a while I glimpsed a smudge of dust on a distant ranch road created by a vehicle on an errand.

When I drove along the west-facing edge of field, Pikes Peak—cool-looking, weather-making, bulking—spiked up into the horizon. In every direction, unvarying flat countryside encouraged my thoughts to wander along aimless paths. The pitch of engine noise changed to reflect minor topographic bumps and dips as the tractor bounced and bucked and tugged with relentless, methodical strength, dropping thousands of tiny seeds into shallow trenches on each pass.

Eventually, the drill bins emptied. To resupply I drove to the side of the field with the big, high-sided grain truck, its red box brimming with a dune of wheat berries.

The only reasonable way to transfer a large quantity of seed from truck to bins is to climb in and shovel. A pebbly quicksand, the wheat berries gulped me in to my crotch, from which position I scooped big bites over the edge into the waiting empty drills. The seed held the movements of my lower body down to a slow-motion swim. I twisted and dug and poured out the humble commodity that all the effort and expense and complicated economic web depended on.

The rationale for winter wheat hangs on the notion of getting a jump on spring. In theory, the seeds, planted in late summer and fall, receive enough water to attach toehold roots which eventually push up short, green, vulnerable sprouts. Then, the plants lie dormant through the winter cold. On good years a blanket of protective, water-promising snow covers the fields. Whenever the growth signals arrive in spring, the wheat crop is ready to take up where it left off, shortcutting the growing season.

I took up the monstrous circles again, sweating in the heat, wheat berries in my pockets and shoes, dragging a pastel brown cloud of topsoil behind me, driving in a slowly tightening spiral toward the center of the field.

The first day ended without calamity of any sort. I parked the tractor, the truncated furrows an unfinished sentence, and drove away feeling much the farmer. Beginner's luck.

On day two my ignorance and carelessness very nearly brought down the whole enterprise.

Needing fuel, I followed Norm's instructions: filled the rectangular gas tank in the pickup truck, charged it, laboriously hand-pumped seventy-five dollars' worth into the bottomless tractor tank, and started up again. Only, something bothersome niggled away at the back of my mind, some essential part to the picture gone awry. Perhaps it was the sound of the engine dieseling along.

"Diesel!" I realized out loud, with a mental jolt that included a vivid image of myself indebted for life over a rebuilt tractor motor. "Jesus, I filled the damn thing with regular!"

Nearly half the morning down the tubes rectifying that near miss—siphoning off fuel, filling every gas receptacle on the ranch with the excess regular, so I could return to the gas station with an empty tank and charge another bill for a load of diesel.

"You idiot!" I kept muttering.

Back to the planting, trying to finish the field before Norm came back wondering why it'd taken so long to do so little. The tractor that had become a benign iron horse suddenly reverted back to a vehicle of forbidding value and power, a machine that I controlled by thin reins and a weak grip. All afternoon I toiled around the hot field, never again quite as confident or assured as I'd allowed myself to get on the first day, until the final strip of latent wheat lay in the ground and twilight tinged the horizon.

More fields waited, more hot crawling days under the sun, sheathed with the topsoil I raised, alone but for the predatory hawks that circled in the tractor's wake like sea gulls behind a fishing trawler, waiting to pounce on the gophers and mice turned up in the earth-opening trenches.

I'd been trained in intellectual problem-solving at college, even used it as a teaching tool with students. I'd grown to relish fresh challenges in that familiar territory. But on the ranch, the problems confronted me out of an unfamiliar milieu, stymied me repeatedly in ways that stomped flat my college-educated ego. I stumbled over infuriating little things out of ignorance and lack of experience, things that relegated me to the level of a grinning clown when someone more seasoned came along and solved the difficulty in thirty seconds. Like the time I ran out of gas in the ranch pickup while one tank still registered full, because I'd only flipped the dashboard switch and hadn't known to turn the valve lever on the floor. That cost me a two-mile walk and a goofy, rueful head shake to the neighbor who stopped by and figured out my gaffe before I even finished explaining the problem.

September days slipped past and Norman visited me on the job, visibly impatient to get all the seed in the ground. He refused to take the time to fix a radiator leak in the tractor, so I stashed jugs of water in the cab and in the grain truck and stopped every two or three turns to refill and pour in another vial of some leak-stopping additive that proved less and less effective as the hot days persisted and the radiator holes enlarged.

But each evening when I finished I'd look over the acreage I'd planted and feel a swell of pride. Standing on the top step of the tractor, I could almost sense the potential there for life and growth, the thousands of seeds bedded in the combed earth, all of them planted by machinery I controlled. The furrows followed the contours of small valleys and hillsides, the lines unintentionally artistic.

On the summer's final circle of wheat, the metal tongue connecting wheat drills to tractor snapped. For an hour I jacked it back up, tried to re-rig the bolt holes, even made a desperate attempt at splinting the heavy bar together with metal fence posts and wire. No go. After a mile-walk to the nearest vehicle and a call to Norman, followed by a three-hour delay until he arrived, I spent the rest of the afternoon waiting for a ranch neighbor to show up with his welder so we could get on with things.

Norm's impatience level rose as visibly as mercury in a thermometer, but by that time I'd worked for him long enough to develop an immunity to his high-pressure vibrations. A month earlier I'd have been pacing and fretting alongside, but I'd grown mental callouses to match the new gnarliness of my hands. I'd waited for him enough times that I found it amusing to watch him get antsy.

Besides, I'd learned the role of the ranch hand who has done everything in his power. In the frenetic round of summer jobs, a rest was rare enough to cherish and use, whatever its cause.

"What plans do you have for winter?" Norm queried abruptly.

"Nothing definite." I sorted through some of the possibilities as a teacher that I'd been half-heartedly courting. Most of those leads had turned cold, either through circumstance or my own inattention. "There are a few things I'm working on," I finished.

"Well, I'm still thinking about cattle. Have to see how prices go."

For a minute the conversation lapsed. Norm worked dirt from under his thumbnail with a pocketknife. A breeze rustled the cottonwood leaves in a tree that bordered the ranch house driveway.

"I'll need someone to live out here if I buy." He snapped the short blade shut. "Should know soon."

Then he returned to the present. "Where is that guy?" He stood up and leaned on the engine hood of his car, rapping knuckles on the metal as he thought about everything slipping behind schedule.

Suddenly he turned again and faced me.

"When's your next rent due?"

"End of September."

"Why don't you move into the ranch house?"

When he saw me mentally turning over the thought, Norman continued, "I'll pay you five hundred a month and free housing. I can't promise how long it will be. Still haven't committed to buying cattle, but as long as winter holds off there'll be work. You won't have to drive, and you'll save on rent."

"Can I think about it?" I couldn't resist making Norman wait.

"Let me know tomorrow."

Little Horse Creek

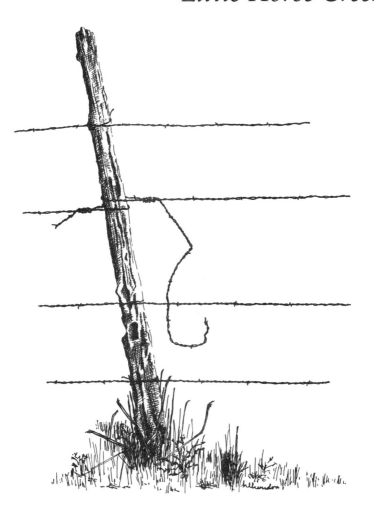

T he tractor breakdown shortened my work day. By the time we'd finished welding the tongue, evening approached. I might have gotten in an hour or two before dark, but Norm roared off toward town and I found myself wandering down the ranch road, considering the latest job proposal. I headed for the creek wash east of the house.

The first time I had really noticed Little Horse Creek, Steve and I were bucketing across the wash in four-wheel drive on a hot, breezeless August afternoon. Checking and repairing fence lines had us in a prickly mood, hardly susceptible to environmental beguilement.

"If Steiger had just given us new goddamned wire, we could have been done with this job days ago!" I reworked a theme we'd been harping on since the first broken length of fence.

The ranch pickup, another vehicle grown prematurely old and beaten through rough use, another vehicle with violated exhaust system, spun and roared its way up the steep sandbank of the creek, fence posts skittering across the truck bed, wheels slamming over the top hard enough to make me duck to avoid the metal roof.

Conversation with Steve was limited to the general unreasonableness of our work, the inhospitable nature of summer weather, and his vacation fantasies. "When I get enough bread," he confided, "I'll take the old lady and drive to a beach somewhere. Maybe Texas. Lie around and drink beer. Stay as long as the money lasts."

A grove of tall, rough-barked cottonwood stood up-stream, a rare fund of shade. Out of the corner of my vision, I saw a large bird beat its way silently through the trees and away over the open plains, rousted by our clamor. Owl, I thought, a big owl. I marked the place mentally.

Cozied up at the edge of trees, the remains of a farm-stead hinted at possible scenarios resulting in abandonment. An unused but still serviceable windmill stood motionless in the heat; pipe hung over the rim of a leaf- and dirt-filled tank as if panting. A tumbleweed-occupied lean-to opened onto what once had been a small corral. A square concrete foundation outlined on the ground the shape of an old home.

I might have chosen this tucked-away spot to build on, I thought, imagining myself arriving at newly claimed land, overwhelmed by the frightful labor ahead of me, the scent of failure nestled inextricably in with the hopes for success and permanence.

We continued with fence-building and other jobs. The memory of the cottonwood grove receded until I went that way again on my evening walk. I indulged an impulse to explore and climbed through the three-strand fence.

The owl again confirmed its watchfulness by winging away at my approach. This time I was waiting for it and identified it as a great horned. Standing in the center of the overshadowing cottonwoods, ankle deep in dead leaves, I spotted the owl's nest, a large platform of twigs and grass and leaves anchored at the fork of a substantial branch. Pellets of regurgitated matter on the ground revealed, in the matrix of bone and fur, a diet of mice and small rodents.

A twin-track road led into the farmstead past a neatly closed gate. I followed the old tire tracks and balanced on a corner of house foundation, trying to recreate the floor plan. A small place, three or four rooms—perhaps an upstairs with a bedroom or two, but more likely just one story. An old outhouse leaned crookedly into the hill to my left. One or two charred pieces of wood made me wonder if a house fire had dealt a blow too cruel to recover from. Or had difficult years simply piled together until the excruciating reality of failure became unavoidable?

I pictured a couple seated at a small kitchen table, hearing the faint creak of the windmill through an open window, leaves whispering in the trees, aware of their tiny light in an unpopulated sweep of land, trying to talk their way around crisis. The man paces to the window, the room too small for him, railing against their bad fortune and unrealized potential, dirt-cracked hands jammed into his pockets. The woman I imagined seems resigned, afraid to confront the choices, bent-shouldered in the face of overwhelming odds.

They look young but weathered and hardened by adversity. Their faces are lined with strain and the effects of sun and wind. The woman's hands are chapped and dry. She rubs them slowly together as they talk. She watches her hands move against each other as if absorbed by them. The sound they make is an arid whisper. The way the couple interacts implies that this conversation is an old one, that nothing personal is meant by the more heated exchanges, but that they need each other to stake out the arguments. Trapped, defeated, bitter, angry—they alternate between fighting and comforting.

The fencing and corral and sheds indicated that they lived there for some time. I wondered if they'd had to travel to the foothills to gather the poles for the corral fence. Sections of the small enclosure had collapsed; rusted sheet metal warped upward from the lean-to roof. I tried to see the structures new, to sense the sounds and smells of penned livestock, to feel the warmth of life. The animals would have been close enough to the house to hear. The woman would tend to the feeding and watering while her husband worked in the fields. She would blunt the edge of lonely unvaried hours by talking to cattle or sheep, checking on the chickens that roamed the yard in search of bugs and seeds.

In the dry creek bed I discovered pieces of a small dam and the pitifully tiny, bone-dry basin behind it. Perhaps the settlers used creek water for the livestock and to water a small garden plot. The sand wash looked as if it never ran full. I wondered how deep the cottonwood roots had to penetrate for water, how often they endured without it, whether the trees were responsible for sucking the sand dry.

The gently sloped valley angled up toward the planted fields, enclosing the pocket of trees, pressing around the spot that hinted at available water. Short grasses, invaded by a species of prickly pear cactus, grew on the valley sides. The natural vegetation appeared even sparser than normal, and I interpreted the density of prickly pear as a symptom of overgrazing.

The day's warmth lingered in the grove; occasional puffs of wind made the old windmill clank faintly, accenting the quiet. A flicker flashed on red highlighted wings through the shadowy cottonwoods.

I sat on a small stump—tree felled for fence posts, firewood?—upstream from the farm site. I wondered what had lured the young couple to the plains. Had they been enticed by overzealous relatives? In the early days of settlement, railroad handbills had touted land that didn't need to be cleared, virgin soil that required only the slightest encouragement to burst forth with crops. Town developers and

railroad outfits flaunted pictures of proud farmers staggering under the weight of monstrous loads of produce. These
salesmen made glowing claims without shame.

I thought then of the pictures I was familiar with,
taken during the dust bowl in Oklahoma, Kansas, eastern
Colorado, when the brutal truth of drought and hail and
wind and bitter winters had hit home. Black and white pictures. Men and boys fleeing to shelter through clouds of dust,
wind tugging at their hats, a terrified dog in the background,
tumbleweed caught in midhop, pitiful lean-to structures
behind them—lean-to structures like the one I could see before me in the still, evening light. The faces in those pictures
are gaunt, dust-sheathed, constricted. The people are an
indeterminate age. But the eyes express a numbed state of
shock, the inner hunger of desperate times, and an odd mixture of anguished loneliness and pained shyness.

Land that never needed to be cleared. Think what that
must have sounded like to people in Missouri or Pennsylva-
nia. Sod that had never been turned. New earth waiting to
accept productive seeds. Only when they arrived, when they
had no choice but to carry on with their decision, would
reality slowly strike.

Homesteaders faced the same problems as early explorers, only they somehow had to make their living in that
inhospitable land. How does one build a house, make fences,
provide heat without wood? Where does a steady and de-

pendable supply of water come from in an environment that receives less, often much less, than twenty inches of moisture a year? How does one find shelter from wind and storm and heat in a shelterless land?

Desperation spurred invention. Farmers chiseled fence posts out of limestone, planted thorny Osage orange hedges to corral livestock. They made do with sod dugouts that were little more than oversized gopher burrows. Dark, tiny rooms crowded with too many people, susceptible to being buried under snow drifts. Mail-order house kits were offered to those with any wealth.

If they were lucky and had extra money, they might dig a well to tap the underground supply; but usually they walked miles for water. Fuel for cooking fires and heat had to be hauled great distances. Men made seasonal pilgrimages to the mountains with wagons to cut timber. Much of the time children were sent out with gunnysacks to collect cow chips.

Settlers existed on hardtack and pinto beans for months on end. Scurvy was not uncommon. Some were reduced to collecting the green young shoots of Russian thistle for their vegetables. "Starved out" was the familiar stark phrase that explained many of the abandoned homesteads.

My thoughts returned to my own decision. Was Norman luring me out to the ranch like a modern-day town developer? Would the work last? Even if it did, was it work

I wanted to do? I knew I wouldn't face the same difficulties as early pioneers. I could drive to town for diversion, go to Rush for dinner, call people on the telephone. But it would be quiet and almost certainly monotonous. I knew that no matter what, my ranch occupation wouldn't last long. Much as I was learning to enjoy the land, challenging as the different jobs were, it wasn't my long-term direction.

The cottonwoods were turning to gnarled silhouettes in the darkness. The angular shapes of the small structures in the shadow of the trees had softened. I started walking back toward the ranch house. Moving through the dry leaves in the grove, out to the road, I heard the scurrying movements of rodents, the subdued calls of birds settling in for the night.

Truth was, I already lived on the ranch in every way but mailing address. Although the job had never been anything other than temporary, as one task hooked up to another and I learned my way around the new territory, my interest in pursuing other avenues paled and retreated. I had no telephone in my apartment, knew none of my neighbors, spent no time there except to sleep. Consciously or not, I had attached myself to the plains environment and took pride in mastering the frustrating but satisfying work.

Little Horse Creek

Manitou Springs never really enticed me on any level. The town clung parasitically to Highway 24, luring tourists and residents with cog railways, tacky gift shops, and restaurants that either belonged to formula food chains or strove to emulate them. Some evenings I walked around the gaudy town, listening to snatches of tourist conversation, and felt loneliness of a quality that never overtook me on the barren space of the plains.

People who lived in my apartment block, a stockade of one- and two-room efficiencies that enclosed an asphalt parking area, were obvious transients. Not tourists; transients. They couldn't afford the Manitou Springs diversions, drove beat-up secondhand cars. Some wore the cropped hairstyle that marked them as recent Fort Carson discards. Others prized a Harley-Davidson the way more affluent individuals might aspire to a Jaguar. Perhaps I reacted unfairly, but I never felt inspired to knock on doors to introduce myself. Every week another tenant moved in or out. My neighbors clearly felt as much loyalty and sentimentality toward their living quarters as I did.

Each day I unwittingly brought plains souvenirs home with me—topsoil, wheat berries, farm-truck engine grease, fence post splinters. More significantly, I increasingly returned with mentally captured treasures as well—hawks hovering over a field, the luxurious sound of water gushing from a sprinkler, the stun of quiet that strikes when the tractor shuts down for the day.

My hands had grown calloused and scratched and dirt-creased from manual labor, my face and arms developed a deep brown farmer's tan. I visited a friend in Denver who hadn't seen me since before I'd begun the ranch work, and I could see the shock register at the sight of my darkened, work-hardened transformation. And I realized that in spite of the tenuous nature of my position, the flippant attitude I had begun the job with, I'd shed a layer of apathy, like a transparent snake skin.

I'd been in the ranch house only a few times on errands, filling water jugs or making a phone call, never with an eye sharpened by the thought of living there. At the end of my walk I took a short tour. One stuffed Salvation Army–vintage armchair and a small white kitchen table with two wobbly chairs comprised the entire furnishings. In the glare of the kitchen light bulb I could see old muddy boot prints marked across the linoleum. An unplugged refrigerator stood agape in the kitchen. The inevitable summer dust coated everything thickly.

I stood at the stained porcelain kitchen sink and looked out the window, across the dirt parking area to the shadowy bulk of weathered barn, past the pile of alfalfa pellets, into the dark space I knew to be a circle of newly planted winter wheat. I had planted that field, knew its boundaries, its views, its slight topographic nuances.

Inside the house the motionless air captured the day's heat. Noisy flies butted against the windows. The image of my dreary Manitou Springs efficiency came to mind, accompanied by my sense of isolation and restlessness when there. But I also entertained the prospect of real isolation, aloneness, that would be my life in that empty, creaking ranch house. I considered having to move again in a month if Norman chose not to buy cattle.

The next morning I told him I'd live at the ranch.

Plains Home

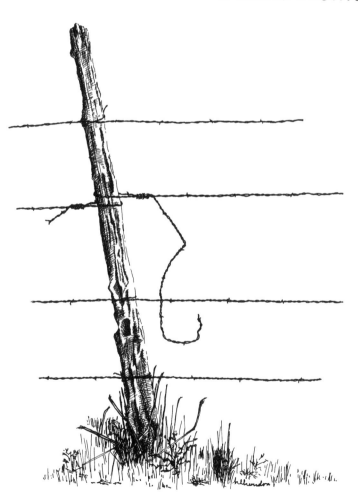

A ll of my belongings easily fit into the bed of my pickup
truck. I'd made the drive from Manitou Springs many
times, but on moving day I noticed certain details with extra
clarity, marking the occasion's significance.

The land looked to be on the cusp of seasons. Summer warmth still pulsed life into crops. Sprinklers stood out
like metallic insects, some still spurting water. Fields of
nubile winter wheat pushed up green shoots, but mowed
wheat and alfalfa lay drying in rows or stood baled and
stacked in autumn-colored cubes. The anvil-hard heat of
August had softened to a more temperate warmth.

I tried to assess my mood, traveling past landmarks,
seeing the few cafes, bars, and gas stations that would
be incorporated within my circle of activity. I looked for
the one or two people I'd met on errands, but saw no one
familiar, even recognizable, in the little towns that flashed
by. It felt nothing like a homecoming; my budding attachment didn't warrant such familiarity. I approached the new
phase more as a pioneer, with tension underlying anticipa-
tion, more as if I were setting up a seasonal encampment in
risky territory.

Scattered fall drizzles and one or two cool, overcast
days had nudged Norman's anxiety index up a notch. He'd
include the ranch more frequently in his flurry of obliga-
tions, pummeling me with chores and long-neglected details to tie up before winter.

"We need to lay some wire before the ground freezes," Norman told me on arrival. "I'm renting a 'ditch-witch' for the afternoon. Unload your stuff and start on the trench. Go from the new irrigation motor to the pivot."

I had committed myself full-time to the ranch, but Norman retained his day-to-day approach to my duties. I still had only a vague outline of my responsibilities for the upcoming weeks, and waited each morning for the revelation of the latest challenge. I felt like an explorer who could see his map only in daily sections.

Within an hour my possessions had been swallowed up by the spacious house. My needs would be adequately met in three rooms—kitchen, bedroom, storage room. In the living room, I deposited an ancient Webcor radio and record player, my home entertainment center complete with mono sound and a playing needle with the heft of a small nail. Everything else fit, with room to spare, in the front half of the house. I plugged in the empty refrigerator and escaped the oppressive quiet.

For the remainder of the day I wrestled with the aptly named ditch-witch, lining out a trench for electric wire deep enough to be safe from plows. Lowering clouds threatened rain. Rocks and summer-hardened earth resisted the gnawing metal teeth under my grip. I underestimated the distance from motor to pivot. The open horizons and lack of objects by which to gauge perspective repeatedly fooled me into underrating spaces on the plains, even at close range. Hour after hour I glanced over my shoulder and thought my goal no closer.

I'd read that Zebulon Pike had first seen the peak that came to have his name from some distance, and thinking it close by, took a party to climb it; several days later, they were still approaching the mountain, and ended up climbing only a minor summit before turning back.

A new sense of aloneness invaded my thoughts, heightened by the gray clouds, the tedious solitary work, the unavoidable impact of my move. When Norman drove up to watch me finish the less-than-arrow-straight trench, I welcomed his company.

"Any rain?" he called.

"Not yet."

"Damn. Showers all around, but none here." He climbed through the fence, careful with his clothes. "The ground needs moisture." He scuffed at the dirt. "Two years ago we had a beautiful crop of wheat ready to combine. Prices were even up. One day before we cut, a hail storm beat it all to hell. One field over, nothing even got touched."

"Fickle," I said.

"Fickle, huh? More like a pain in the butt!" He eyed me wryly. "Moved in?"

"I guess you'd have to say so." I thought of the cool, too-roomy house, thick with dust and unstirred air.

───────────────

— ⁓

After work I drew a hot bath. My arms were covered with dirt and still quivered from the vibrations of the heavy machine. The water ran rusty out of the tap for a long time before it cleared the pipes, but the bath's warmth soaked off layers of dirt from my skin and I lay there until it cooled.

No food, I realized. The Rush Cafe beckoned from eight miles away, and I closed the door on the house with relief, escaping its cheerless confines. I pulled up in the ranch truck, tools and jacks jumbled in the bed, de rigueur fuel tank and hand pump snugged up against the cab, matching company with the other trucks parked off the highway. Despite wearing the correct uniform and having earned my weathered look, I entered the cafe knowing how little I shared in common with the people there.

Conversation lulled at my entrance, heads turned, eyes assessed, then talk resumed. I slid onto an orange, vinyl-covered bench at an empty booth. A waitress took my order—rancher's daughter, young wife, I couldn't judge. Friendly enough, but not inquiring, more involved with the other patrons. I watched her lean toward the conversation of two older men on her way to place my order.

They seemed to communicate as much by subtle gesture and knowing look as by words. Their hats rested on chairs, but the sweat-darkened hat-band mark stood out clearly around their heads. They ate methodically, steadily, until their plates were utterly clean.

My appetite was genuine as well. Rural food—meat loaf, mashed potatoes, canned vegetables, gravy, washed down with a beer. Human company, however removed, provided comfort. I lingered, ordered pie, listened to the sporadic discussion revolving around who had their hay up, whether rain looked likely any time soon, what feeder cattle were selling for. People glanced my way once or twice, and when I left, toothpick between teeth, another single man just going out gave me a miniscule, acknowledging nod.

To postpone closing myself into the ranch house, I used the remaining daylight to prowl through the barn and corrals, poking around the compound of buildings and machinery. The barn had been long unused. Boards hung loose, the roof sagged, swallows flew in and out through the many structural gaps. Old straw and dried manure lay scattered on the floor of the stalls. Any animal smells had been leached from the building. In a cement-floored workroom, several tin cans containing assorted screws and bolts lay on a bench, a rusted pair of fencing pliers hung on the wall, some ancient straps of horse tack dangled like discarded leather belts from nails. I kicked a red tobacco can clattering across the room. The noise startled me like a shout in a library.

A lean-to roof extending from the barn was stuffed to the rafters with tumbleweed that had found peace from harrying winds. I thought about rattlesnakes in the thorny nest of dry twigs. A large empty water tank made from a hoop of corrugated metal sat at the edge of the biggest corral, a corral that would require substantial attention before it would hold any four-legged creature with a yen to wander.

Except for the freshly painted tractor with its drills and discs, and the red grain truck, everything in the ranch yard possessed an atrophied, forlorn look. A comically optimistic mailbox, the size of a small wheelbarrow, had been anchored confidently on a pillar of masonry that would have taken a bulldozer to knock over. I could likely have stored two year's worth of letters there, at the rate I expected correspondence.

Shrubbery planted in a thick screen blocked the white house from the road and north winds. Two or three large cottonwoods grew randomly around a yard that hadn't been graced by a lawn in years, draping their branches over the high roof. Across from the parking area, a conical pile of alfalfa pellets, looking like feed for a race of monster hamsters, stood in a sharp peak.

I walked under the kitchen window, giving the white ranch truck a thump with my fist. As I entered my new home, the pump motor engaged from inside the well house.

The air inside hadn't been made mine. It still hung trapped and stale, negatively scented. I played a scratchy Linda Ronstadt album on the Webcor while organizing my things, hanging a picture or two. Two sides of the record allowed ample time. I tuned the radio to a powerful station I'd discovered on the tractor radio while driving in circles: KOA in Denver. It featured livestock prices, weather reports, sports call-in shows, traffic updates—an appropriate agenda for ranch life. The announcer's voice boomed through the house.

Worn floral carpet in the living room gave away the walking patterns of former residents. The other floors sported cracked and chipped linoleum. The surfaces sloped and humped as if the extremes of temperature and years of neglect had played havoc with what once was level. Most doors needed planing. On the north side, a screened porch with green indoor-outdoor carpeting opened toward the dirt road and shadowed fields. A set of sturdy hooks in the ceiling suggested the need for a broad swing, a cool summer seat from which to digest supper and contemplate work, watch the play of light on the land, wave to infrequent passers-by. I noticed that the yard light had warmed to full power, triggered by darkness, in company with other widely spaced ranch lights shining forth every few miles like dryland lighthouses.

The phone hung on a kitchen wall, and on the windowsill next to it lay the thin directory; in spite of its modest bulk, the book covered a vast area of eastern Colorado. Addresses for ranches were vague in the extreme—N of Ellicott, SW of Yoder, and so on. Steiger ranch rated a listing, SE of Rush, pinning my location down to a quadrant of land as undefined as it was expansive. The few Yellow Page listings concentrated on tractor sales and repair, well drilling, combining services, irrigation outfits, and stockyards.

I swept up the kitchen floor, making a pile of dead flies, dirt, and old scraps of phone-message paper. Boredom and an unwillingness to contemplate the future drove me to bed early.

A streak of warm weather sparked Norman to command a flurry of season's-end chores, none of which turned out to be as straightforward in practice as in theory.

First, a sprinkler had mired itself in mud of its own making, and had to be jacked up and freed. Sprinklers run a close second to barbed wire in the amount of trouble and frustration they cause. To begin with, the cost of pumps and pipe and center-pivot machinery runs into the hundreds of thousands of dollars by the time you get a few systems placed on the fields. Then, with discouraging regularity, pump motors break down, or the water coverage is uneven, or the irregularities in a field screw up the way a machine moves. By the time you notice a problem, half a day or more might have gone by, time in which you've either lost that much watering exposure or drowned a section of field because the sprinkler has been stuck in one spot, methodically gushing water.

This one had stuck and then created a sea of mud. Several of its metal wheels had become mired a foot deep in ooze. Since then Norman had let the machine sit, and the mud had hardened to concrete. I had to chop each set of wheels free with a pickax, jack them up, and insert a platform of heavy boards underneath so they could roll to freedom. A half day's worth of grunting, cursing, improvising toil, none of which a college education prepared me for, took care of that small chore.

For two full days after that I painted the underground pumping station at the origin of Norman's waterline. The experience gave me an appreciation for the claustrophobic existence of submarine crews. A circular hatchway just above ground level, much like that on a submarine, gave entrance down a metal ladder to the subterranean throbbing heart of the waterline. An intimidating array of gauges, power switches, and electric panels confronted me with choices I felt relieved not to have to make.

The heat from the working engines was so intense, I might as well have been working in a sauna. When I began painting, asphyxiating fumes combined with the heat in the tight, ventless chamber. I related to underwater crews waiting for depth-charges, breathing air with less and less oxygen. With increasing frequency, I stumbled topside to the wash of fresh air, to the relief of a broad horizon.

The image of myself succumbing to the infernal conditions, passing out beneath a stretch of cheerfully painted pipe, where I would lie for days before being discovered, assumed the proportions of a phobia. My visits upstairs lengthened and came at closer intervals. Each return to the Dante-esque depths required more vigorous self-flagellation.

"How much are you paying me?" I asked Norman when I confronted him next. "Forget it. It's not enough."

By mid-October Norman had run dry of errands and still hadn't decided whether or not to buy cattle. Life on the ranch settled to a subdued pace. Most days were mine to do with as I wished. A skeletal routine took shape.

On Tuesdays the Rush Cafe served homemade doughnuts, sugary confections hot from the fryer. It seemed that a number of people adjusted their schedules to arrive at the cafe when the doughnuts were fresh. Salesmen parked their shiny passenger cars alongside the usual farm vehicles. Telephone service crews, tool belts jangling, hard hats on the floor next to their chairs, took over a table and busied themselves dunking doughnuts in mugs of coffee. Nearly every week I noticed the same four older ranchers at a table under the front window. Their conversation was too low to overhear, but I sensed the long view of local history in their confidential chuckles, the careful looks they gave new arrivals.

Bored by my own company at lunchtime, I often drove in for the daily special—pork chops, meat loaf, ham, potato salad, jello in orange or lime-green squares—all for a couple of dollars. I remained shy about asserting myself, rarely said more than a few words, and no one there came more than half way, socially.

"Who is that guy?" I imagined the waitress asking the cook after I left.

"I dunno. I think he works at the Steiger place. That's who he charges gas to anyway."

A local poultry farm sold eggs out of the drink cooler at the front of the cafe. Ninety cents for a cardboard flat of thirty. I soon adopted a monotonous, high-cholesterol breakfast habit; the eggs tasted better than any I could remember.

Most evenings I ate at home, enduring the ordeal of cooking for myself, eating at the rickety kitchen table, usually finishing in under fifteen minutes. Then a ritual walk across fields or down the road to Little Horse Creek. Several times I rode my bicycle on the dirt road, cringing when trucks passed, the astonished faces of passengers turned back toward me. On ranches, people quit bike-riding around the age of thirteen. I figured that the vision of an adult man pedaling around alone on the dirt roads likely provoked speculation about my political beliefs and other, more deviant social behavior.

In my spare time I explored the contours of ranch property by truck, justifying the activity by cursorily checking fence for breaks and sags. At under five miles an hour, it was a form of motorized pacing. Pasture angled disjointedly around fields planted in alfalfa, maize, or winter wheat, the crops fenced off protectively against the unrealized threat of cattle.

A windmill or two sprouted above ground, poised over shafts leading down to ground water, ready to pump up a column of fluid when freed to accept the wind. The simple technology and ingenious design of windmills always struck me as particularly satisfying, especially when compared to the fuel-guzzling, high-priced equipment agriculture generally depends on.

Sprinkler systems and their stubby, gray electric motors stood out as jarring metallic disruptions against the horizon. No wonder they were frequently struck by lightning. Little-used wheel tracks led to water tanks or circumnavigated the borders of field. In the distance, a row of power line towers led off out of sight.

The angular, inflexible, confrontational structures created by man, even the houses that stood out squarely to face the wind, symbolized to me the contrast between our approach to the environment and that of the natural vegetation and wildlife. Where we make things that won't bend, flexibility is a necessity for trees and plants. Where our structures stand out harshly, wild animals blend in and utilize natural cover to hide their movements. Where we attempt to force nature to comply with our will, plains life has developed adaptations and life strategies that are appropriate to the requirements of the land.

Several stacks of hay bales, the shape of immense, squared-off loaves of bread, two hundred feet long and twenty-five feet tall, were piled at the crest of a low ridge.

"Two dollars a bale, or forty bucks a ton," Norman had told me, in case anyone came around wanting to buy hay.

Except for the deep green of winter wheat shoots, autumn colors dominated the land—dried maize stalks, brown shortgrass pasture, sand in the washes; even the leaves on the cottonwoods by the house had begun to turn and wither. The tender carpets of winter wheat always struck me as out of place, tragically unnatural, as if by biological error the plants had gotten the seasons wrong. The look of those fields evoked the same emotions in me as the thought of an orphaned fawn, going into its first winter alone and vulnerable.

Prowling innocently around the borders of Steiger property, I stumbled into an occasional embarrassing adventure. On one pass, a length of old barbed wire somehow wrapped itself firmly around the drive shaft of the farm truck, winding up into a huge knot, like a metal goiter. Louder than usual clanking and mechanical complaints woke me from my meditations. Investigation turned up the thorny spool, along with a hundred-yard tail I'd been dragging around the fields, bedecked with tumbleweed, tussocks of grass, old cow chips—farm ornaments.

At least I usually suffered indignity alone.

On another warm afternoon, I lazily opted not to lock in four-wheel drive to get across a sandy wash, and promptly went axle-deep in a dry quicksand. Even in four-wheel drive, the only way I finally extricated myself was to jack up the rear wheels, place boards under them for traction, lurch forward a foot or two, and repeat the process ten or twelve times.

Mid-October. I succumbed to the temptation of the Rush Cafe at suppertime, sat, as usual, alone at a booth. Slow night. The waitress moved into the kitchen and I listened to the rhythms of her conversation with the cook without hearing the words. An older couple at a table hunched up around their cups of coffee, stared vacantly at the salt and pepper shakers, and spoke hardly at all. I heard the slapping of a fly swatter in the back room, somebody excited to predatory action against the hordes of lethargic houseflies that decide every fall to come inside.

Three bicyclists pulled up in front, leaned their bikes against the building wall below the front windows. I turned to look when I saw the waitress's face at the order window, brow puckered with interest. The older couple roused, shifted, turned halfway in their chairs to gawk.

Two men and a woman stood outside, pulling sweat-stained riding gloves off their hands, stretching, rummaging in their panniers for wallets and clothes. They looked hesitant about coming in, and when they did the three of them stood in a tight cluster just inside the door for a moment, checking the room, before moving to a round table with red-and-white-checked plastic tablecloth.

With a boldness I never displayed around local customers, I approached their table and asked if I could join them.

"Where are you going?"

"Los Angeles," one of the men responded, "if cold weather holds off long enough for us to get south."

They had begun their trip in New Jersey, had been deserted by two members of the original group. "I don't think they realized what they were getting into," the woman explained.

They extolled the friendliness of people they'd met along the way, recounting the many acts of hospitality and generosity they'd benefited from. Wind and heat had been their consistent foes across the midsection of the country. "Some days we could ride only early morning and late at night."

"Where do you plan to stay tonight?" I asked.

They looked at each other. "Don't know," one said. "Usually we find a park or ask if we can sleep in somebody's field."

"I live down the road," I continued. "It'd be backtracking a little, but we can load the bikes in the truck and I'd bring you back here again in the morning."

I recognized the bikers as closer kin than the usual cafe goers, realized that as much as I was offering them shelter for the night, I pursued them for their company, a diversion from another uneventful evening at the ranch house.

They accepted my offer with alacrity. The older couple turned to watch us depart, the waitress stayed at the cash register while we hoisted bikes into the cluttered pickup bed and crammed, thigh to thigh, into the front seat.

For one night I played the part of resident and host in a place where I usually felt the foreigner. Driving home, I pointed out property borders, identified cattle breeds, described a few of my work misadventures. I led a brief tour through the ranch buildings, got my appreciative visitors up into the tractor cab, like city folks at an agricultural museum.

We stood in the yard and listened to the twittering of a passing flock of horned larks.

In the house, I saw them take in the hermitlike furnishings, the dearth of utensils, lack of pictures or flowers, the extent to which my occupation of the building resembled a bivouac. Gear mushroomed from their panniers into a colorful clutter. We played records and shared adventure stories while the trio took turns soaking in hot baths, tended to bike maintenance, wrote in trip journals.

The next morning I fed them farm-egg omelets and drove them back to the pavement. They wrote down my address. "We'll send a card when we make California."

The woman gave me a kiss on the cheek, and I saw that she recognized the fact that instead of my sending them off, they were leaving me behind.

Patterns

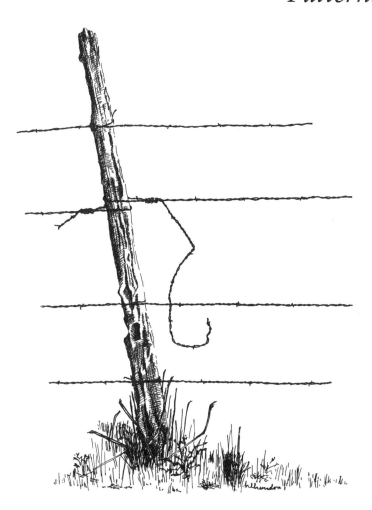

In the early weeks after my move to the ranch I fell prey to the temptation of taking trips to Colorado Springs on flimsy pretexts. The transition to a solo lifestyle made me seek some vague reassurance. I responded by gravitating toward concentrations of humans, as if proximity to hordes of strangers would erase my sense of vulnerability. A drive in for fencing supplies or machinery parts provided the excuse to return to the city and treat myself to a restaurant meal.

I'd eat alone, observing the fashionably-dressed business executives at lunch, the manic conversations at crowded tables. My work clothes suddenly seemed shabby and soiled. I perceived a quality of derision in the glances I caught from other tables, as if I had hay stuck in my hair. I preferred the frank, uncommunicative stares I received at the Rush Cafe. Soon the appeal of those visits lost its pull.

My last tie to the city was through a medical technician's course I had enrolled in before the ranch job started, a certification I'd thought would strengthen my job qualifications, but which had little application in my current situation. Once a week I drove in for the evening class. More and more confident in my grasp of the ranch road network, I eschewed pavement in favor of dirt. And I drove at a slower and slower pace, more of a constitutional than a commute.

The small towns along Highway 94 had a feeble life-pulse, but they throbbed with activity compared to the real back roads. I passed abandoned one-room schoolhouses, the siding weathered gray, weeds and thistle grown over the play yard. Rural crossroads might not see a dozen vehicles a day pass through. Snakes could safely sun on the roads for hours. The roads meandered in and out of sandy valleys, past short-grass pasture where distant Herefords plodded after food and water, through one or two shady groves of cottonwoods.

Sometimes I stopped and turned off the engine. I could distinctly hear the ripping sounds cattle made, pulling at dry tufts of vegetation fifty yards away, the clack of grass-hopper wings, the caress of evening breezes feeling across the miles.

Where pavement began, I quickened the pace, my trance broken. A discernable tension would creep into my posture and I wouldn't relax again until I made the return trip, well after dark. Then, ranch lights that winked in patterns like fallen, far-flung constellations guided me back. I considered the families signified by each light, the clusters of buildings and machinery, the individual fires of aspiration and dream symbolized by each pool of illumination.

My truck rattled along at the front of a cloud of dust, headlights exposing fence posts and telephone poles, the startled eyes of cattle, the ghostly beating wings of birds of prey. I got so I could pinpoint my own yard light from a dozen miles away, home in on it as if it were a navigation beacon, and then wheel up to the deserted house, silence and darkness crouching on the edges of the lake of light.

Patterns

At times I fought through periods of restlessness and boredom brought on by reclusive living. But I also responded to the cadence of exposed and uncluttered days. I felt as if I inadvertently approached some inner source of power and strength, living introspectively, wandering internal alleys in hours of quiet time, existing in a subtle yet power-laden place.

After dark, I dragged the heavy armchair into the lighted kitchen and propped my feet on top of the propane heater while I read or worked out crossword puzzles. Sometimes I stood at the kitchen window, gazing sightlessly past the harshly lit ranch yard, mentally rambling, tapping the well of my imagination. Weeks might pass between times when I'd sit down to write, but then inspiration fired by the look of the land or the impression made by a local event would expel itself in furious scribbling at the white, wobbly table.

I'd go a day or two at a time without speaking out loud, and my voice would startle me when I next talked into the telephone or met a neighbor. But an internal dialogue wove itself through the time, a subconscious river of thought and reaction and fantasy, a delving into self.

In restive moods I listened to live broadcasts of Denver Nuggets basketball games on the radio, pacing back and forth, living room to kitchen, kitchen to living room, falling victim to the frantic excitement fanned by the announcers.

Half a dozen times a night I might go out the back door and stand in the yard, studying the dense dome of stars for Orion or Cassiopeia, listening for coyote yap or owl hoot, but most often, letting the soothing gulf of quiet lap around me.

Even at night I could sense the rampart of Pikes Peak to the west, shouldering abruptly out of the plains, jutting into the sky, cutting out a quadrant of stars with its dark mass. During the day, I studied the character of sky focused around the peak. Clouds gathered and dispersed, sunrises lit the snow and rock like orange and gold floodlights, thunderstorms roiled blackly there while I enjoyed empty blue sky from where I watched.

In late October the first snowstorm blew in across the plains. I had sensed the change in meteorological mood for days. Where usually I would have flushed larks and sparrows out of the grasses when I walked, I saw no life in my wanderings. Like living barometers, the birds and animals had felt some environmental alteration of pressure and hunkered into their safe places.

Patterns

Pikes Peak was obscured by black clouds. A towering anvil-shaped thunderhead rose above the mountain like a second majestic peak. A dark mat of overcast sky advanced from behind the ranges. The air felt still and poised, breath-held, expectant.

During the night the first snow fell, wet, clinging, blown by a strong north wind. By morning a small drift had worked in under the crack at the bottom of the back porch door and the screened windows had been stuccoed solidly with snow.

More weather marched in from the northern expanse, herded by the close-pressing wind. No work. I drank coffee and tea, cozied up to the heater with a book, made hourly circuits through the house to check the various views of thick weather. A white-crowned sparrow clung to the bark of a juniper outside my bedroom window, snuggled on the lee side of the tree at the base of a branch, its feathers fluffed up so the bird appeared twice its normal size.

By midafternoon I could no longer tolerate my spectator status and responded to an unnatural urge to feel the storm firsthand. Pushed by wind and driving snow, I let the forces take me south past the barn, into a field of winter wheat. Snow lay in a heavy wet pack on the grooved field. Dense clods of turned-up dirt crumbled underfoot. I turned to look back at the house and discovered myself at sea in an obscured, featureless world. Snowflakes stung my face, wind roared past my ears, gray clouds and swirling gusts limited visibility to a hundred feet. I stood alone in a monotonous circle of flat, furrowed ground, cut off from the warmth and comfort I knew lay close by.

Having planted the field, I knew the landmarks and borders, but the storm shortened my view, altered the look of things. Half an hour outside was enough to soak my pant legs with melting snow and burn my face red with the wind and cold. On my return I followed my directional intuition, wondering what I'd do if I missed the house, until the barn loomed up out of the mist, sudden as a ship coming through fog.

The snow melted the next day. I could almost hear the roots of winter wheat sponging up moisture after weeks of too-dry weather. The brown dirt road appeared first, like a pencil line drawn across the countryside. Moisture-laden tumbleweed sagged against fence lines, a sage thrasher ran ahead of me on my walk to Little Horse Creek, and I spent longer than usual at the farm site, following animal tracks like a detective after murder clues, smelling the rare rich dampness of earth and leaves in the air as the snow disappeared.

What had begun as an indulgence of curiosity that first evening trip to the creek wash became a significant element of my routine. Usually after supper, binoculars in hand, I'd cut across pasture toward the building ruins that lay hidden from view until I crested the angled lip of valley.

Bands of plains-hued mule deer sometimes grazed in and around the trees. I never saw them elsewhere on the ranch, but their narrow, hoof-scarred trails wound in and out of the grove. Where they camouflaged themselves the rest of the time I never discovered, but as many as nineteen of them congregated at dusk in the valley, twitching with vigilance, vanishing like dusty smoke to other havens when they detected my presence.

Twice I glimpsed the furtive bushy shapes of coyote slipping away down the sandy wash. When snow covered the ground, an astonishing number of tracks revealed the oasis-like attraction of the sheltering grove for wildlife: small dog-prints of coyote looping and tacking on sensory excursions, the cloven hooves of deer, stodgy scratchings of skunk, stick-drawing bird feet wandering after seed, the feathery darting trails of field mice, and the ominous wing print of owl terminating one of the mousetrack lines with poignant scurrying marks. At night, when I heard a coyote chorus, I pictured them clustered in the valley, their sharp assertive voices cocky under the cloak of black, starry sky.

The fact that wildlife congregated at the grove justified and fortified my own attraction. The rustling stand of trees, the hint (rarely confirmed) of available water, drew life toward it. A comparative outburst of growth—shade, shelter, water, security. The farmstead settlers had chosen it, the austere plains animals made it their local focus, and eventually, I responded as well, with the regularity and need of a churchgoer.

Little Horse Creek gave out hints of its importance in minute fragments, circumstantial evidence. I followed the light network of deer trails, found the flattened circles of grass where they bedded down. I broke apart owl pellets in search of clues to a life and death drama I almost never glimpsed firsthand. Now and then a small puddle of water formed in the reservoir basin, water that appeared mysteriously as an expression of unseen underground dynamics.

The great horned owl became the symbol of the place. In time, I found that a pair of them resided in the cottonwoods, foraging over the fields after their prey, always watchful, the dominant full-time landlords. If I missed seeing one of the dark, silent birds in their place, it made that visit incomplete; their routine had become incorporated into mine. Even away from them I often thought of the soundless power and economy of their flight, the simple predatory nature of their needs, the innate patience with which they bided time. I wondered how long they had held their claim to the cottonwoods, whether they had raised and sent off broods of young from that nest, how far they ranged in order to satisfy their hunting needs, whether they would hatch young that year.

The evidence of human use around Little Horse Creek also illuminated only the edges of a picture. I could have pursued the full story behind the homestead and have uncovered its history, but I preferred evocation, preferred my imagined versions of small-scale tragedy, the anguished couple coping with defeat in the kitchen.

I began, in an odd way, to look forward to my evening visits almost as a social interlude. Perhaps as an antidote to socially barren days, I communed with the couple my imagination had placed on the farm site. I never gave them names, never spoke out loud, but much of the time they resided in my thoughts. I plumbed their motivations, developed their plans and projects, created a relationship between them, felt that I came to know them in ways I couldn't know the real people I encountered.

As my attraction to the land emerged, Little Horse Creek became a symbol for the qualities of the High Plains. Explorers like Zebulon Pike and Stephen Long had viewed the expanse of flat, semi-arid land between the Mississippi River and the Rocky Mountains as a barrier. Early maps refer to the region as the Great American Desert. The lack of wood, scarcity of water, and exposure to weather made for a crossing marked by danger and hardship, a crossing not unlike an ocean voyage. The scope of horizon-bordered, sky-domed space *is* oceanic, and fields of grass in a wind evoke unavoidable water and wave images.

It was then, and for many people remains, a space to get across as quickly as possible. Even if physical danger is no longer a concern—interstate highways having replaced wagon ruts and horse trails—debilitating boredom is brought on by the seemingly endless number of flat miles required to get across Kansas, Nebraska, Oklahoma, or eastern Colorado. Before taking the ranch job, I had suffered from the same syndrome.

The pattern of American settlement reflects this sentiment. The Oregon Trail fed people to the West Coast, to a land with dependable rainfall, flowing rivers, stands of timber. Only later, grudgingly, because the frontier was filling up, did people come to the plains states west of the hundredth meridian. Colorado became a state in 1876, eighteen years after Oregon gained that status.

Even now, the challenge of the plains is as much a mental and emotional test as a physical struggle. People who arrived from the East, accustomed to unbroken forests and lush vegetation, confronted a sere and brutal land by comparison. Without the psychological comfort offered by natural shelter, early settlers suffered from a brand of mental exposure. All the environmental elements on the plains attacked them with the same vehemence with which they erode isolated columns of rock or unvegetated ground. Wind and blizzard, lightning and hail, stupefying heat, numbing cold, tornadoes—difficulties and threats as unpredictable as they were certain.

Patterns

Victories won with unimaginable effort could be snatched away in an afternoon by a chance hailstorm or a devouring cloud of locusts. Standards of living, by necessity, were rudimentary for plains dwellers. Even at that, the framework of life stood as precarious and fragile as a bird's egg in a ground nest. No wonder the stories of mental malaise and shattered hopes are as numerous as the tales of success. The wonder is that people actually stuck it out, weathered the hardships, and found ways to cope, even to thrive.

Some folk thrived because the plains are a perplexing contrast. Harshness is set off by an astonishing fecundity. I had been startled by Norman's ability to supply water to a major city from beneath land that appeared waterless and arid. Given the right strains of dryland crops, enough water, and a dose of good luck, food can be raised on that ground with a vengeance and on a scale matched by few places on earth. That potential and promise holds people, sways them into gambling such high stakes. In humans the dichotomy of the land's threat and its beneficence is mirrored by a strange mixture of hope and fear, optimism and resigned acceptance of fate.

Advances of recent decades go a long way toward mitigating hardships. Telephone contact with neighbors, electricity, access to building supplies, the technology to tap groundwater—all have contributed to the present, relatively secure settlement of the High Plains. But no modern convenience can remove the wind howling across miles of emptiness, the threat of storm and insect infestation, and the inescapable sense of vulnerability like a mouse beneath a hawk, that one has on this vast bench of flat land.

The tales of hardship and disappointment and disaster have not dissolved under the onslaught of technology, either. Softened, yes, transferred in many cases from physical disaster to financial disaster. But they lurk just as menacingly on the edges of existence.

Another unexpected aspect of the High Plains, an aspect I identified at Little Horse Creek: beauty. The allure of the High Plains quietly infiltrates one's consciousness. Mountain, desert, or lake and forest environments strike you with their natural jewels in ostentatious ways, flaunting their wealth. Snow-capped peaks, alpine meadows waving with wild flowers, towering walls of multi-hued sandstone, prodigious waterfalls are scenery highlights that are hard to miss, even if you're traveling at highway speeds. Their attributes are almost confrontational. Look at me!

But the land of eastern Colorado does not shout for attention; its ornamentation is understated and spare. Beauty is more likely to be defined by quality of light, an engulfing stillness, or surprising appearances of wildlife: a fox slipping across the road in front of your headlights, the penetrating and fearless gaze of a hawk on a post, the quick coordinated flight of a band of pronghorn.

In a setting that proffers little and demands a great deal, you earn the random glimpse of beauty, the treasures of its landscape, by living there. The moments of delight and power can be as startling as an unexpectedly brilliant smile on a plain face. As seasons slip past, you find yourself slowly and slyly entranced, grudgingly won over, seduced. And you discover unlikely spots of refreshment.

The dry mecca in Little Horse Creek was mine. Other, more bounteous settings have the endowments to entertain on their own, providing all the sensory stimuli. The secrets of the plains demand a commitment from the observer to unlock the doors of imagination. Little Horse Creek is the kind of place travelers would drive past without giving it a second glance, but I discovered its rewards hint by subtle hint, season by season.

In the geography of eastern Colorado, the dry wash plays a minor role. I never saw flowing water in the creek bed, although it must run there periodically to erode its channel. The arms of Little Horse Creek converge like branches of a huge, grounded tree with Horse Creek and run in wobbly, sandy lines south and east, growing in size and volume as tributaries join in, until they add their force to the flow of the Arkansas River. Other drainages (also usually dry) trend roughly parallel to Horse Creek—Black Squirrel Creek, Steel Creek, Rush Creek, Sandy Creek, Pond Creek—all giving their meager wealth to the dominant, snow-fed flow of the mighty Arkansas, a river endowed with adequate volume to withstand raids of evaporation and demands of irrigation en route to the Mississippi.

Even the bounty of the Arkansas is periodically threatened by the thirst of agricultural irrigation. In drought years lower portions of the river can dry up altogether. Colorado and Kansas have fought for decades, like bickering neighbors, over the right to divert water, a right that literally spells the difference between agricultural success and failure throughout a vast corridor of farmland. In 1949 Congress allocated 60 percent of the water rights to Colorado and 40 percent to Kansas, but that ruling is presently being challenged.

Watershed divides on the plains offer another lesson in subtlety. Just north of the Steiger ranch, across land with no apparent high point or change in slope, the small streams—Badger Creek, Deer Trail Creek, Bijou Creek—flow north, scratching out a similar dendritic pattern to the Platte River drainage.

While eastern Colorado is reputed to be utterly flat, it is in fact wrinkled and seamed with watercourses, and the land actually slides determinedly downhill along with the rivers. Erosional outwash from the Rocky Mountains lies in a broad deep wedge, thickest at the foothills of the Front Range, a mile high, gradually tapering off to the east, leading in a gentle, 800-mile decline to the Mississippi River. At the eastern border of the state, rivers have already descended more than a thousand feet from their levels at the edge of the mountains.

Travel posters displaying Colorado's attractions concentrate on the Front Range metropolitan areas, the condo-infested ski resorts, the clear mountain trout streams. Only the five-minute agricultural report on early morning radio reminds Coloradans that the eastern plains comprise a solid third of their state. Once across the Colorado border from Kansas or Nebraska, motorists expect to be immediately awed by mountainous skylines, forgetting that it takes half a day to get across the flats.

In the vast, dry, often maligned plains environment, myriad secret places like the cottonwood grove on Little Horse Creek go unnoticed and unheralded. Owls nest and hunt from their shelter, coyote gather in nightly wild song, mule deer graze at dusk, and once in a long while a human will stop in such an oasis as well, and be entranced by its spell, unexpectedly invigorated by its beauty.

Little Horse Creek was my secret. The wildlife, the ghosts, the knowledge I gained there filled the solitary time, provided grist for the mill wheels of imagination. I did, however, have occasional visitors at the ranch house, usually someone stopping to inquire about hay. I learned the rural habit of keeping a pot of coffee on the stove.

A man rarely brought his wife with him, and if he did, she usually stayed inside the idling truck while he negotiated. Without the enticement of coffee I had no reason to invite anyone into my austere quarters. When people did come in, they would peer around at the spare furnishings, wondering what sort of situation this was.

"Married?" they'd invariably ask.

"Nope."

"Mmmm."

The men generally remained taciturn, reserved. They'd pull up in a flatbed or a pickup. Then, looking about discerningly at the dilapidated barn and tool sheds, they would walk around to the back door with the high-heeled, bent-legged walk engendered by years of wearing boots. Faded blue jeans or large overalls. Faces marked by the pale and tan hat line. Hands rough as fence posts when we shook. A tendency toward flight in their demeanor, a slight sideways stance, as if ever ready to walk away.

"That hay for sale?" They'd jut a chin in the general direction of the stacks, two miles away.

"Forty bucks a ton."

"Mmmm," shifting feet, a squint around. "Guess I need a couple of tons."

"Care for coffee?" I'd lure them in.

There was something almost painfully polite in the character of these men, as if they felt they might be demanding too much of my time. Often they acted as if coming into my home was an intrusion, invariably taking off their hats when introducing themselves. They listened with an attentive concentration when I spoke.

In time I identified customers—a dairy farmer from near Ellicott, a neighbor to the south with a new shipment of cattle, a rancher from over by Punkin Center who was caught short by the dry weather and needed a few bales to tide his Herefords over until sale day. Men who laid their hats on the table, sat stiffly in the wooden chair, worked their coffee cups between chapped hands, gave little of themselves, and inquired even less.

"I'll help you load up," I'd offer.

Stacking hay into a pickup truck bed is an art. Done right, a tall load will ride sturdily in place, held together by the strength of cross-tied bales, even if they overhang the edge of the bed substantially. Done wrong, the rectangular bundles tumble off and explode on the first corner or bad bump.

Wearing worn work gloves to protect my hands, I'd clamber to the top of the stack, work each seventy-five-pound load loose, and toss it down to the truck below me.

"Ever find rattlers nested in them bales?" one man yelled up to me conversationally. After that I pried into the stack with a new alertness and caution.

"Kinda light aren't they?" a buyer might angle for an extra bale or two thrown into the ton. Or, "A little mold around the edges, isn't there?"

A couple of times a week Norman stopped by to check in. It became clear that more than keeping an eye on the ranch, he needed to get away from the demands of business and town life. He escaped the reach of his nagging car phone, the agitation of bankers and utility commissioners, forgot momentarily the badgered life.

"No TV?" he observed. "Not a bad idea. Don't know what my kids would do without television, though." There was a pause while Norm looked over my setup. "Quiet out here."

"Once in a while, too quiet." I set coffee in front of my boss. "Mostly I like it, though."

"Might have to up the price of hay." Norm veered into ranch talk. "I heard they're getting seventy dollars a ton over in Kansas. Dry weather and poor crops. People running low on feed already."

He would visibly relax into his chair, unbutton his coat, stretch his legs, sip coffee. "Nice here. Sometimes I think I shouldn't live in town, but I got too many things going. Wife wouldn't want to live here anyway."

Patterns

I'd never been to his house, but I knew he lived in some new subdivision cul-de-sac, on a street with a ridiculous name. All the streets had names like Serendipity Circle, Enchanted Avenue, or Tee-time Lane hatched out of the imaginations of some saccharine advertising team.

"What about cattle?" I broached the subject that my future turned on.

"Got a guy down near Lamar checking on feeder sales," Norm asserted, a line I'd heard before. "Pretty sure I'm gonna buy, but I think prices might drop a little more." He looked less comfortable now that I'd brought the pressure of my own concern to bear, another detail to fend off.

"Before that, though," he straightened up and worked his coattails into place, "I've got some more work lined up. In a week or so I want you to go help out near Lamar on some land I own."

"Doing what?"

"Building fence." He noticed my pained look. "Mostly rounding up cattle. You can stay part of the time with a family we've got on a ranch down there. Get the cattle lined out for winter. Might learn something."

Helping Out

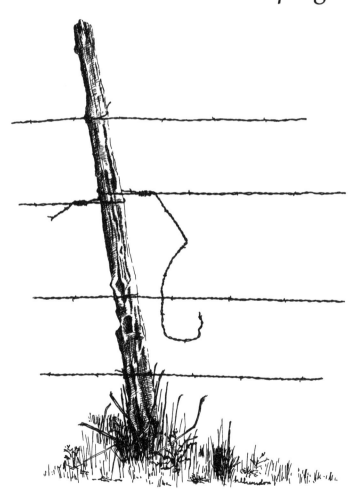

Helping Out

November 1st, my birthday, turned out to be a long and lonely day. Norman directed me to drive to the southeast corner of Colorado, within hailing distance of Kansas, to lend a hand on several large chunks of property he owned. He furnished me with another in his series of skimpy penciled maps, dependent on one or two prominent landmarks—grain elevator, ranch gate, unique mailbox—which, if missed, would throw me off for hours.

The weather was gray and cold, clinging but dry, with a biting wind. The ranch truck ran fitfully, running fine for a few miles and then wracked by stuttering paroxysms, like an old-timer with smoker's hack. Wild Horse, Kit Carson, Eads, Wiley—not the sorts of towns I looked forward to breaking down in.

The ranch I arrived at that afternoon was deserted. I was to stay in the sparsely furnished house trailer. Wind whistled under the metal eaves. I stood in the yard and looked around vainly for orienting topography. Autumn brown land spread in every direction like a table top. The cold penetrated my clothes. In an attempt to avoid a lonely evening, I drove the hiccuping truck thirty-five miles into Lamar and ate at a pizza joint, a place that only accentuated my solitary status and without the compensation of good food.

After relocating my turnoff and finding the dark house trailer with my headlights, I settled down to read a book I'd brought along, *Welcome to Hard Times*. Then the power went off. For half an hour I groped blindly around the walls in search of the breaker box, finding every sharp-cornered object in the place with my shins, and finally gave up in frustration. The only bulb that worked was the one in the refrigerator.

So I ended my birthday by drawing up a box in front of the open, empty fridge, my right side bathed in cold air, reading *Welcome to Hard Times* in the soft, weak glow of a forty-watt bulb.

For a day I fixed fence lines on the land around the house trailer. I had become expert with fencing pliers and kept the tool tucked in a pocket of the saddle-blanket seat cover in the truck. Staples and handy bits of wire lay in the next pocket. Crimping, snipping, tying off, and tightening had become so routine that I could identify a problem and rectify it by rote. I spotted most shorts in electric fence line from the cab of the truck.

But it was lonely. Not socially lonely, like eating at the pizza parlor or living in Manitou Springs, but rather, vast, engulfing, wind-bitten, no relief aloneness. I took to humming tuneless, self-verifying ditties. The space made me feel small, puckered-up, weightless. I lost sight of the house trailer, not behind any ridge or valley but over the curve of earth.

Helping Out

The monotonous horizons of far eastern Colorado made me realize what a balancing and comforting influence Pikes Peak lent to the land I'd grown accustomed to. The mountains served to fix one's bearings, to relieve the flatness. Away from it, I saw how psychologically soothing the conspicuous topography was.

On the eastern border, every view swept away in unvarying fashion to a distant meeting with sky. Widely spaced river beds, islands of cottonwoods, or steep dry washes provided the only noticeable changes and visual refreshment. Until the subtle landmarks on a piece of property seeped into my subconscious (a process that required more intuition than memorization) the sun offered the only hope of orientation.

The agricultural pioneers along the border with Kansas would rarely have caught any glimpse of mountains. Everything that would have been difficult about homesteading closer to the Front Ranges would have been doubly so here. Water would have been scarcer, wood farther away, sun and wind and blizzards more fierce, the howl of a wolf or the dry rattle of a snake more threatening. The border country had the feel of midocean: no end in sight.

I was relieved to move on to another place, this time south of Lamar, to help with the cattle, a job involving other people. I hardly minded sleeping in a musty, wind-rattling sheep herder's trailer, listening to mice all night.

At 5 A.M. dawn signaled its arrival with a tinge of gray in the eastern sky. Horses and men moved in shadowy silence through the corral, breath smoking. The creak of saddles and the chink of bit against horse teeth, the grunt and mutter of someone cinching a girth, the stamp of a hind hoof on hard ground.

We paired off to begin rounding up a widely dispersed herd of cattle. "You two go to the southeast corner and work back toward the middle." The ranch foreman pointed to me and the partner I'd just shaken hands with in the darkness.

Pickups pulling double horse trailers clattered off to disparate points of open plain. *Southeast corner*, I thought. *Work back toward the middle!* I was in the habit of using distant peaks to orient myself. The dynamic sky over mountain ranges functioned as a meteorological barometer. The interplay of cloud and peak even provided me with some subtle entertainment. Here, except for the generalized tint of brightness in the sky, nothing served as a navigational aid. Nothing. *This is what a solo sailor would feel like just after he'd dropped his sextant overboard.*

I didn't own cowboy boots, had to think about how to mount up, gave away my inexperience by my tendency to bounce in the saddle. I trusted the horse's instincts more than my own and hoped the animal wouldn't take advantage of my insecurity. I stuck out as the college type who didn't know much that was useful, but I managed not to embarrass myself badly. The other men commanded their mounts, riding with the same nonchalance with which they drove pickups. My partner and I moved slowly back and forth across the vaguely lit range, hunched into our coats to ward off the cold, rousting cattle out of washes and from behind clumps of frosted sagebrush, prodding them to their feet, shouting to make them move.

"Hey, cattle! Hey!" The cows shook their heads and mooed, necks stretched out, reluctant as school kids on Monday morning. "Hup, cows! Hey, cattle!"

Slowly we gained a herd, our horses pushing relentlessly from behind, our shouts less necessary, animal inertia building up. By the time the sun had worked up through the atmospheric haze, we joined with several other groups. I took a position to the rear and on one side, content to plod along and watch others charge off after escaping cattle. My own horse seemed half asleep, as if he knew his rider wouldn't demand much. The land looked dry, tufted with cropped-down clumps of grass, the rocky soil sprinkled with prickly pear cactus.

Several older men rode together, their conversation broken by short exertions after straying cows. Another cowboy rode by himself, slouched in the saddle, perhaps recovering from a hangover, head nodding. His reverie ended abruptly when a prankster gently lassoed him from behind and gave a sharp tug, yanking him partially off his mount.

"Wake up, bub!" The foreman rubbed it in. I quickly checked behind me.

Hours later the cattle sensed the corral coming up and jostled toward it, ignorant of what awaited them. The horses pushed harder, ready to be rid of their riders. Dust rose in a dry, chalky cloud, stirred by thousands of hooves. Riders galloped ahead to open gates and turn the herd in.

The foreman's wife waited in a truck next to the corral, a huge urn of hot coffee and a tray of homemade doughnuts on the open tailgate. She had gotten up well ahead of us that morning to make a whopping farm breakfast—eggs, oatmeal, sausage, bread, bacon. Then, still before dawn, she got her two kids onto the school bus they rode two hours each way to town and back. After providing our coffee break, she would return to the house to finish preparing dinner. On normal days, when neighbors weren't around, she worked the cattle and helped her husband with heavy chores.

The herd milled and bumped together in the contained space. After the coffee break, cowboys waded amongst the agitated animals, sorting cows from calves and yearlings, waving arms, spitting tobacco juice, chasing after strays in a hobbling, bandy-legged jog.

One large calf refused to be separated. It successfully eluded three or four winded men, squirting jets of green shit in the effort, until the whole group of us were enlisted in the chase. Predictably, the take-down came to me. Sprinting alongside the frightened calf, I launched into an awkward neck tackle, hanging on like an overmatched linebacker atop a lumbering fullback, until we went down in a bawling tangle of hooves and legs. It earned me points for gusto, if not finesse. As I dusted myself off, someone suggested I join the rodeo circuit.

That year's calves hadn't been branded, and I spent the balance of the morning on the ground, kneeling on calves' necks, holding one front leg in a tight, immobilizing bend, while another cowboy controlled the hind end. A third man jockeyed the metal irons in and out of the propane heater tube and burned the ranch symbol into the flesh of the helpless animals.

Sulfurous smoke from burning hair rose in rank plumes. I turned my head away to breathe. The sound of flesh being seared and the panicked convulsion of animal under my knee signaled the end of another branding.

"These damn cows don't even feel it," the man wielding the irons said as he watched a freed calf scramble off, bawling. "Their hides are thick as an old elephant's."

I nodded my head, but felt the contrary evidence squirming beneath my hold, watched the rolling white eyes, heard the frantic calls of calves in shock.

Young bulls required the extra measure of castration, an operation performed by pocketknife. Periodically we dipped the blade in alcohol. The pairs of testicles were collected in a nearby bucket, thereby transformed into "Rocky Mountain oysters," a plains delicacy. The branding man placed an occasional ball on top of the heater tube and cooked it there, rolling it along. Corral hors d'oeuvres.

By the time we'd finished with the calves, the foreman called dinner break and the group filed into the small house, stomping boots and dropping hats on furniture. The meal was a minor orgy of consumption—several kinds of meat, vegetable dishes, bowls of salad and jello, casseroles, homemade bread, cold cuts, and a row of pies for dessert. Conversation slowed to grunts and gestures and complimentary mumblings.

An inane game show droned from the television in the next room. I heard waves of manic applause and contrived frenzy over the clank of utensils and sparse talk. The television played all day, like background music in a doctor's office. The only reading material I'd seen anywhere in the house was some old *Reader's Digest*s in the bathroom. A citizen's band radio crackled on the windowsill, tuned in to over-hear distress calls from nearby ranches and to communicate the mundane daily messages back and forth from house to truck.

A neighboring rancher named Bud pushed away from the table and patted his shirt-stretching belly. He squinted as he lit up an unfiltered cigarette and exhaled a shot of pale smoke.

"I hear old man Curtis' place is going up for sale." Bud snicked at his nicotine-stained teeth with a toothpick. "All his kids have growed up and gone off."

"Can't blame them," the young foreman added. "That place hasn't made money in probably fifteen years. What kind of future is that?"

"Shit, who *has* made money?" Bud snorted smoke. "Without crop subsidies and Uncle Sam's drought relief we'd all be broke."

"Seems like all the young people are going off." It was the first thing I'd heard John say. He was the oldest member of our crew by a long shot. Gray hair, a deeply creased face, a lean look. I'd noticed how he always seemed to be in the right place on a job, yet never hurried.

Everyone nodded, worked harder with toothpicks.

"Even if you inherit a place from your folks, a fella can't hardly be sure of making it." This from the cowboy nearest the radio. "With what a bushel of wheat goes for you'd be better off plowing it back under than taking the trouble to sell it."

"I don't believe a young person could get a start without inheriting land." John neatly swept together the last crumbs from a slice of meringue pie. "Nobody I know's got that kind of money."

As if at a prearranged signal the men made their way into the living room and sprawled around on the floor or in chairs, groaning audibly, settling in for a siesta like satiated snakes after that month's meal. Conversation ended. The television droned through the afternoon game shows.

I considered the resigned tone of the table talk. It struck me that I'd met very few young people in my ranch work. From what little I'd been able to gather from the workings of the Steiger operation, it was small wonder that newcomers found it nearly impossible to get a foothold.

I thought about what it would take to get established. Even with government help—payment-in-kind programs, disaster relief, crop subsidies—the financial burden is staggering. Acreage, machinery, irrigation pipe, sprinklers— dollar amounts into the millions are common. And that's the ante, getting into the game. To stay in you have to keep up. Buy seed, feed for livestock, fencing supplies, gasoline. Maintain equipment. No end to it. All with no guarantee that prices will remain stable or some disaster won't wipe you out along the way. Norman had told me once that farmers and ranchers are the only business people who buy retail, sell wholesale, and pay the freight both ways.

The catalog of potential calamities waiting to derail you would be enough to create a neurotic out of a calm man. Blizzards, blight, locusts, drought, fickle markets, flood, hail, sick livestock—all crouch at the edge of possibility, unpredictable predators waiting to pounce. It's a rare year that doesn't include one major misfortune and a host of minor crises.

Ironic, I thought, looking around the room, that these men who relished their independence and ability to solve their own problems also represented one of the most dependent sectors of society. I was certain they would all bristle at the brand "socialist," yet socialist is what agriculture has become. "Communist" would be an even less popular label, but communal labor was exactly what we were practicing. The scale of work involved in producing crops and maintaining livestock herds can be as overwhelming as the required capital investment. An eight-hour day is often logged before noon during the busy times.

Modern and expensive equipment has eliminated some portion of the manual labor, but the periodic spates of heavy work still require extra manpower. At branding time, haying time, calving time and roundup time, neighbors gather into a communal work force to get the jobs done. The men stretched out around me received no compensation beyond the knowledge that they, in turn, would be the beneficiaries another day.

That and the chance to see other people. Most of the year the families are spread widely across the plains, living isolated and insular lives, separated by intimidating distances, preoccupied with unending chores. Spending a day in good company, even hard at work, would have the same sort of reviving effect as a rare trip to town would have for early settlers.

My meditations had become more and more dream-like. My eyes closed and the sounds of the television faded into the background. But as I drifted toward real sleep, the foreman grunted and heaved to his feet. "Well, boys, there's a herd of worried ladies waiting for us."

Within minutes everyone had stretched, reclaimed his hat, once again thanked the foreman's wife for dinner, and headed back to work.

The afternoon's work entailed checking cattle fertility and culling out diseased individuals for an early trip to slaughter. There's no delicate way to describe the pregnancy check. One by one, we funneled the cattle into a fenced aisle leading to the squeeze chute, an apparatus that enclosed each animal in a metallic embrace. Each of us was armed with an electric prod to convince reluctant individuals. Some of the men tended to use the shock excessively, with a kind of vengeance.

Without any discussion that I overheard, John was designated as the pregnancy checker. As the group's senior member, perhaps he was particularly skilled at this peculiar specialty. He wore a shoulder-length plastic glove, clipped in place high up on his shirt-sleeve.

With an incongruous delicacy, he inserted his arm up the cow's rectum to a point well above his elbow. Palpating from that internal location, it is possible, theoretically, to actually feel the fetus that is forming in the cow's womb. The method struck me as crude and prone to error, but I wasn't tempted to question it for fear that I might get to try it out.

Understandably, cows react to this violation with surprise and some vigor. Given their position, their only effective retaliation is to clamp down hard with their sphincter muscles. John's occasional grimace attested to the pressure this reaction generated. The enraged cows bellowed their distress. The sharp banging sounds of hind hooves lashing out against the squeeze chute punctuated the general chorus of men's shouts and animal noises.

John, with arm inserted, assumed the preoccupied concentration of someone groping for a hat in a pitch-black closet. The rest of us stood around waiting for his prognostication.

Someone at the cow's head might inject a bit of wry humor. "I think she likes you, John," or, "I believe she's smiling." John ignored the banter. Eventually, the verdict would emerge.

"Pregnant!" as his gloved arm slid out, the squeeze chute clanged open, and the abused cow exploded out to pasture. Those proclaimed "not pregnant!" were led off into another pen and onto a waiting cattle truck, victims of ranch efficiency standards.

Another cowhand looked over each animal for general health as it came through. Some had been lamed by "ski toe," a result of uneven wear on the hoof that causes it to curl back on itself and grow into the foreleg. One or two had a cancerous tumor extruding grotesquely from their eyeballs. Several suffered from advanced cases of "pink eye." They joined the barren cows condemned to shipment.

All afternoon the alarmed and angry cattle filed past, endured scrutiny and gloved penetration, had judgment passed on their immediate destiny. Dust and dry manure settled in a haze through the afternoon sunlight. The sharp smells of sweat and cattle urine filled my nostrils. The last cows suffered their ordeal. The loaded cattle truck rumbled off down the dirt road.

Clusters of men gathered and exchanged final bits of news while they slapped dust from their clothes. There was an air of reluctance about them, as if they wished to linger, despite the long work day. The sun had set, and a gray twilight brought a chilly breeze with it. I remembered that we'd been at the same corral before sunrise that morning. The men dispersed with final waves and joking banter, driving off like scattering atoms across the long distances. They might not see each other again for months. The foreman and

I closed gates in shadowy darkness, made for hot showers and another gargantuan meal that would begin with Rocky Mountain oysters.

Life on the Run

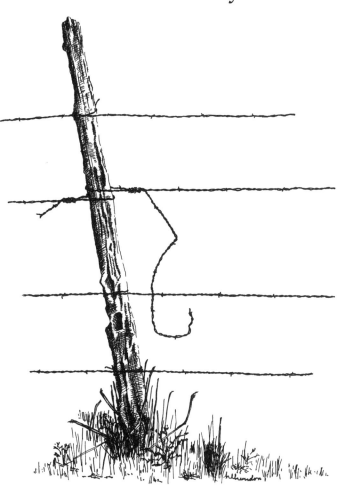

Life on the Run

When I was young I used to lose myself in books about the frontier West. Mountain men and Oregon Trail scouts, restless boys who struck out for the far wilderness, characters I idolized and envied with youthful intensity. The wildness, the space, the ever-present tension and danger had an exhilarating effect on my imagination. I placed myself in those high, lonely settings, felt the winds, saw the wide and unpopulated vistas spreading below some airy perch, views alive with free-roaming animals.

On the Steiger ranch I worked as a cog in the agricultural juggernaut that is largely responsible for eradicating the virgin West. I caught only oblique glimpses of wildlife and faint hints of the days before people crowded the plains—an unfenced view, a high circling eagle, the lash of storm in unsheltered space.

Norman kept promising to buy cattle, but as November flowed by and no herd came to the ranch, I spent more of my time wandering, looking, thinking. The fence lines had been built, the machinery put up for the winter. The fields rolled off in a dry brown quilt, set off by the startling green of winter wheat. I roamed by vehicle and on foot, coming to know each hillside, every wash, the fence posts where I could expect to find a rough-legged hawk.

I spent entire afternoons at Little Horse Creek making discoveries—new birds, a nest in the branches that I hadn't noticed before, some discarded bit of machinery or corroded tool that helped fill in the settler picture. I assumed that the man and woman would have spent much more time together during the winter months. This seasonal proximity would have been both blessing and curse, offering shared time that would have seemed shamefully luxurious in the summer—but also a five-month stretch of unbroken days that would inevitably bring on the waspish symptoms of cabin fever.

I thought through their chores—hauling water, feeding animals, grinding out laundry by hand, baking bread, fixing tack and machinery. Perhaps they read at night, browsed through mail-order catalogs, or wrote letters.

I saw them heading out for a midwinter afternoon walk down the wash, escaping their confining home, bundled in coats, plodding heavily through the cold sand. They didn't speak. Heavy gray clouds clamped down against the horizon. The sounds they made walking were loud in the silence. Once she pointed to a black-tailed jackrabbit that bounded ahead of them around a bend. They had about them an air not of contentment, but of patience, biding time before the anxious season, the time when they'd worry over crops and rain, worry over their ability to succeed, to survive. At the end of their walk they climbed awkwardly up the cutbank and stood together, looking downstream, briefly holding hands, before turning back.

In the homesteading days it would have been impossible to foresee the domination we've come to exercise over the land. Back then the daily struggle just to maintain the essentials of life took all of people's energy and stamina. Clutching to a frail roothold against the punishing elements was hard enough. Our potential to overwhelm, to eradicate entire species, and to till millions of acres would have seemed a distant, unfathomable prospect. But now that far-fetched vision has become stark fact. As a species, we consider ourselves owners of land to an extent that absolves us from natural law. Little as I cared to admit it, I played a part in the rapacious game.

From my position, as much observer as participant in the work of ranching, I tended to identify with the animals who witnessed the human bustle and rampage, and who had no option but to succumb to its dominating influence. The contrast between domesticated animals and wild ones accentuated my sympathetic leanings. Cattle, horses, and pigs plod through their lives, dependent on humans, unwary and overweight much of their existence. Compared to the svelte figure of a pronghorn at a full run, the quick alertness of mule deer, or the cagey watchfulness of coyote, domesticated livestock seem retarded and pampered.

The shift of balance, from grubbing pioneer to dominating landlords took place in the span of two long life times.

Norman's grandparents and the grandparents of men who came to buy hay lived in an era ranch children today wouldn't recognize, an era when humans were more on a par with animals, when the outcome of the struggle for control was often in question.

Intellectually, I knew how completely we'd laid our hands on the plains, but as months passed on the Steiger place I confronted the incontestable fact that my youthful images of the Great Plains teeming with wildlife were obsolete. In the last two hundred years, significantly less than that for all practical purposes, animal life has been brutally pruned from the prairies and plains. Wildlife of the rich and interwoven diversity found in the early 1800s will never return.

But even for those of us not fortunate enough to witness the spectacle of plains animals at the height of their development, the images are difficult to bury. The evocative space remains. I often found myself mentally removing the fences and sprinklers, the houses and power lines to reset the stage.

Bison that covered the plains like an endless moving carpet, a brown shaggy mass of bellowing, grazing, wallowing animals. Packs of wolves that waxed healthy on the fringes of herds of ungulates, feeding on vulnerable calves or infirm adults. Grizzly bear that roamed the prairies as unquestioned rulers of the food chain. Birds of prey, migrating clouds of waterfowl, fleet antelope, bighorn sheep—a bounty of animal life equaled today only in a few shrinking sections of African savannah or northern tundra.

In May of 1804, as Lewis and Clark ascended the Missouri River on a voyage that now seems unbelievably distant, they recorded: "The game is in such plenty that it has become a mere amusement to supply the party with provisions." A few days later they observed that "the game is now in great quantities, particularly the elk and buffalo, which last is so gentle that the men are obliged to drive them out of the way with sticks and stones."

It is hard to imagine that only a few generations after those observations were made, people grow up in the plains states and never once glimpse wild buffalo, elk, or bighorn sheep, much less wolves or grizzly. America's push to conquer did indeed meet with success, but the acrid taste of sadness and shame infiltrates that triumph.

In the early decades of this century, wolves still howled at night in Colorado. But they were attacked with a passion and hatred out of proportion to their actual threat. There is something in humans that needs a demon to fasten on. Wolves were killed throughout the West by the tens and hundreds of thousands, killed brutally and often with stomach-turning cruelty. In amazingly short order, they were gone. The few vestigial pockets of wildlife that remain have been hemmed in, relegated to parks, sanctuaries, and fenced enclosures, more zoos than wilderness. Ironically, they now need protection from the uncontrolled growth of humans.

Permanent dense settlement of the land made the situation irrevocable. Even if we'd like to reverse the trend, wildlife at its former level has been made impossible by our parceling, fencing, plowing, irrigating, and pasturing efforts. Animals that have persevered, the animals that I watched, are forced to adapt to limited and obstacle-strewn environments.

What we now consider normal settlement of the plains is, in an evolutionary sense, a recent aberration. Nevertheless, Norman and the ranchers I met based their assumptions and attitudes on the premise that this state of affairs is the permanent status quo. From that perspective, deer and antelope grazing in fields compete unfairly with cattle. Coyote and large birds of prey are vilified as voracious predators that, given free rein, will decimate stock animals. Rattlesnakes are routinely killed on sight. Talk of reintroducing wolves in the Rocky Mountain West fans the flames of primitive biases. In many places bounties are still routinely paid for coyote, mountain lion, and other "varmints."

If a predatory animal kills our livestock, it is our right to shoot or poison it. If our crops fall prey to insects or disease, we broadcast toxic poisons to eradicate the threat. Hunting quotas are based on our own definitions of overcrowding. Given the human ant pile, wildlife doesn't need to burgeon much to crowd us.

If Lewis and Clark returned today, the transformation of western countryside, the dearth of wildlife, the complete taming of a huge region would astound even those servants of progress. The fact that any wildlife at all still lives on the plains—and in a limited way even flourishes—is a testimony to species' adaptability, hardiness, and survival drive. Successful animals on the plains have learned to cope with the demands of life on the run.

Besides dealing with the depredations of technology and crowding by humans, High Plains animals struggle with fierce environmental difficulties. Using camouflage, fleetness, nocturnal abilities, and astounding skill at finding and utilizing meager shelter, the creatures that have survived civilization go about their business surreptitiously and with admirable economy.

The sight of a band of pronghorn galloping across prairie looking like a school of fish darting through clear water in mysterious coordination, always made me stop and watch in appreciation. They use speed and observational acuteness to assure their safety. Keen eyesight allows them to spot danger at great distances and once in flight, they are capable of speeds of over forty miles an hour, faster than any other North American mammal. Their leaps can cover more than twenty-five feet. But pronghorn are limited (sometimes with dire consequences) by the fact that they refuse to jump fences. I'd catch sight of one wriggling awkwardly under a low strand of barbed wire, a desperate-looking posture for an animal that, at other times, seemed outfitted with springs for legs. If they can't crawl under a barrier, they are effectively barred from travel, and in times of starvation or drought, they may be unable to reach food and water.

Coyote are perhaps unparalleled in their ability to adapt to an environment crowded by humans. Bold, inquisitive, but also cautious, they have spread to almost every North American climate and terrain, even infiltrating the edges of cities and suburbs. Foraging widely, they take advantage of carrion, garbage, plant matter, rodents, and occasional larger game, in an omnivorous and intelligent approach to survival.

Although coyote have few, if any, natural predators, they withstand unrelenting attacks from livestock ranchers. Sheep and cattle farmers are nearly universal in their adamant condemnation of the coyote. Once the wolf had been exterminated, the coyote inherited the most-hated status. Since agriculture has dominated the West, coyotes have been trapped, shot, poisoned, even lured to bait equipped with explosive charges in a persistent attempt to eradicate the species. Incredibly, and in spite of massive losses, coyote thrive in the face of man's systematic attempts to destroy them.

I rarely saw them in daylight. Once or twice at dusk I glimpsed one loping at the edge of an old maize field, its coat the same tawny color as the dried stalks. Sometimes they ran off down a sandy valley when I came near. Most often I heard them at night, barking and caroling under the stars, leaving tracks for me to discover and interpret in my wanderings.

Rattlesnakes compete with coyote for the dubious distinction of being at the top of the High Plains hit list. Snakes and humans have never been particularly chummy, and rattlesnakes carry the additional onus of bearing poison and possessing a startling, paralyzing rattle. Westerners traditionally go out of their way to run over snakes sunning on roads and habitually kill rattlers whenever encountered.

Not infrequently, rodent epidemics beset ranch country. Mice become so thick you can hardly walk outside without stepping on them. Mice drown in wells, raid feed bins, burrow dirt tunnels dense as capillary vessels. The fact that one of their foremost predators, the rattler, has been killed on sight for decades can't help but explain part of the phenomenon.

I didn't entirely escape the local antipathy toward the only poisonous snake in the region. Haystacks, tumbleweed piles, rock ledges—all potential rattler lairs received my careful attention and an involuntary shiver, a primal chill, ran down my spine at the sight of the reptile. But they went their way and I went mine at the end of an encounter.

The black-tailed jackrabbit combines several strategies in order to succeed on the open plains. They stay close to sagebrush and other cover when possible, depending on camouflage to mask their presence. They sleep in "forms," shallow depressions dug to take advantage of a sheltering bush or rock, and economize their water intake by remaining in shade during the heat of the day and utilizing the water content in their forage. When chased, jackrabbits can sprint at better than thirty miles an hour and bound twenty feet or more at a jump.

Birds were the most visually accessible wildlife for me to observe. Not that they have been immune from the impacts of settlement. Hawks, owls, and eagles have long been hunted as pests, seen as predators who kill chickens and lambs, even accused of preying on calves. Waterfowl and game birds like pheasant and quail are shot for sport and food. Pesticides, DDT, and lead poisoning have contributed in insidious ways to the demise of other species.

Peregrine falcons were brought to the brink of extinction because they ingested, through their prey, DDT used in pesticides, which made their eggshells so thin and brittle as to be unviable. Waterfowl populations in some areas have been severely depleted by lead poisoning, a result of inadvertent ingestion of waste lead shot from shotguns. Irrigation has drained wetlands and concentrated toxic elements such as selenium in what habitat remains. The results of these toxins have just recently been recognized. A high incidence of horrible birth defects in waterfowl, defects reminiscent of thalidomide babies, has been correlated to wetland areas high in toxins. Other water birds become sterile as a result of poisoning. Birds such as the Eskimo curlew or whooping crane, once healthy species, are nearly extinct as a result of indiscriminate hunting and loss of habitat.

In spite of these losses, birds tend to be more visible and vocal than other wildlife. I began taking note of my sightings, identifying seasonal comings and goings, reading up on different species' behavior and habits. My observations began as an intellectual exercise, a minor discipline, but evolved into a pursuit of avian companionship. More important than the natural history tidbits I studied, I began to gain some sense of the character and individual personalities of local bird life.

I discovered with pleasure that the great horned owls were likely to be permanent residents; that they often inherit their nests from former occupants, usually hawks or other large birds, and that owls are voracious and efficient carnivores whose dietary tastes include a smorgasbord of other birds, rodents, rabbits, skunks, snakes, and frogs. They hunt in the dark hours, the times when humans are reduced to sensory retardation, and I picked up clues to their nocturnal activities only indirectly.

Once, driving along an empty dirt road, I noticed a large dark figure in a field, the size of a coyote. When I pulled over I identified the silhouette as a mature golden eagle working on a rodent kill it held firmly in its talons. The bird looked sharply at me, but made no move to retreat. Although at some distance, I gathered in the dangerous hook of beak, the piercing unwavering eye, the unequivocal grip of talon in fur. Standing on the ground, the eagle looked huge, a feral power beyond description.

On my back road explorations I regularly spotted eagles. Swainson's hawks, rough-legged hawks, and marsh hawks perched on telephone poles or fence posts, preening their feathers or surveying the ground for the movement of prey. On my more traveled routes I actually came to expect specific birds, and felt let down when they didn't appear.

The sight of Swainson's hawks hovering tensely above the brown cloud of topsoil I stirred up behind the tractor had been an ordinary part of my planting days. Often they swooped down to pick up a startled pocket gopher I'd turned out of the earth. By fall I noticed fewer and fewer of the summer hawks. Within a period of weeks they migrated south toward the plains of South America, replaced in Colorado by rough-legged hawks, birds that summer in the high arctic tundra.

I grew familiar with the look and habits of the larger birds: the tilting low flight of marsh hawks gliding over fields; the wide, flat-winged soar of eagles; the characteristic hovering profile of a rough-legged hawk, wings panting in the dry air, intent on some patch of earth.

Smaller birds attracted my scrutiny as well. Horned larks scattered in front of the truck on dirt roads by the thousands. Loggerhead shrike sat on phone wires with predatory intent. A small bird of prey that makes up for diminutive size by its fierceness, shrike commonly kill birds or rodents by impaling them on thorny growth or barbed wire.

On my kitchen wall I hung a list of birds and other wildlife I'd seen, with a code to denote their seasonal or resident status. I read up on each new addition, fitting the details of life history into the context I'd observed. Once or twice when someone came in for coffee I noticed them squinting at the page, but no one commented.

Among cowboys and ranchers, animals other than livestock were seldom spoken of with appreciation or enjoyment. In a basic sense, living things that weren't worth money were in direct competition with cash crops and domesticated livestock. Their view of wildlife was jaundiced by that adversarial relationship. When they saw a coyote from the road, their first reaction was to grab a rifle from the rack by the back window in the truck cab and get off a shot. They referred to most birds of prey simply as "chicken hawks." When they found a dead calf in a field with coyote sign around it, they assumed the worst, that the young cow had been brought down by a marauding pack, discounting the possibility that the coyote could have arrived after the death occurred.

Not that an opportunistic predator won't take a livestock meal when given a chance, but coyote and birds of prey feed mostly on small rodents and snakes. I never saw evidence of livestock killed by wildlife, and heard of few documented cases. Even if a small percentage was killed by predators, it seems a reasonable price to pay for the larger benefit of keeping rodent and small mammal populations in check.

This animosity isn't evil or even particularly thought out. It comes with the territory. These men aren't cruel. They care for their families, they're honest and unassuming, often good humored. They act on the same ethic that has characterized America as an expanding nation for hundreds of years. But they see themselves as leading a beleaguered existence, already plagued by bad weather, unpredictable markets, and myriad catastrophes beyond their control. To see deer nibbling at a haystack or a coyote feeding on a carcass adds salt to their wounds. Resentment is understandable from an economic perspective.

Only I didn't share the perspective. When I glimpsed the untamed, wary plains creatures I saw grace and beauty and resourcefulness, not inconvenience and threat. I saw life that eked out an existence in spite of us. And I applauded it. If asked whether losing a cow was worth killing a coyote, I'd come down on the side of the coyote every time. Although I participated in the cultivating, livestock-caring effort, I cringed in the face of the unquestioned tyrannical stranglehold the agricultural monopoly maintained.

The Meat Crop

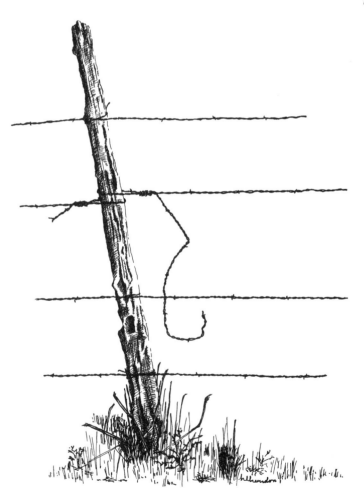

B eginning in late November, Norman finally made good
    on his claim to pasture cattle and some thirteen hun-
dred head were brought in for the winter season. My quiet
roaming time ended. I spent several days in the corral,
frantically working to make it ready: patching gaps, cleaning and filling the water tank, repairing the loading ramp.

Over the course of a few weeks, livestock trucks
thundered into the yard, carrying loads of yearling steers
and heifers, young cattle Norman hoped to fatten up over
the winter and then sell when prices went higher. Each new
group that arrived unloaded in a clattering, bellowing rush
off of the idling cattle trucks. I kept them penned up for
a day or two to make sure they didn't shows signs of shipping sickness, an ailment commonly exhibited by cattle
after the multiple traumas of feedlot, livestock auction, and
transport.

For that time I lived amidst the tumultuous sounds
of young animals voicing their distress. Even inside the
house, the noise penetrated my sleep, like hundreds of
distant bawling children. Wading through the anxious herd,
I singled out those individuals that appeared listless and
runny-nosed; they received shots of red medicine, a general
antibiotic, and extra time for recovery in the barn.

In the evenings I'd climb to the top of the fence to
survey the mass of brown and white bodies crowded in the
dusty, pungent pen. The silent interludes I'd become fond of

abruptly ceased. If I went out to look at stars, the cattle would raise the level of their complaints another notch.

After allowing the animals to settle down for several days, I turned them into the large pasture, where they typically went on a long tour of the periphery. Usually the whole group took a lap or two around the fence, keeping up a steady pace, orienting themselves to new confines like a shipwrecked crew circling an island.

For the first week or so I herded the cattle to their water tank until they memorized its location. In the time it took a new bunch to settle down, obstreperous characters made themselves evident by breaking through fences or testing lengths of electrified wire. Those cattle and I developed a mutual resentment, a combative relationship hardened by repeated battles of will.

The cattle provided work that allowed me to stay on at the ranch. Without them I would have been moving again, thrown back into uncertainty about the future. But I never worked up much affinity for the beasts. Too often my adventures with them were laced with frustration, anxiety, and anger.

Once the cattle had accustomed themselves to their new confines, and as long as mild weather held, my duties amounted to little more than driving the fence line, taking a rough head count, and keeping an eye out for individuals that looked sick. An hour or two a day usually sufficed. Ranch life resumed a lazy pace. Surprises were almost never welcome.

The Meat Crop

Cattle, I came to believe, are just smart enough to do what you don't want them to, but too stupid to figure out what's good for them. I sensed, much of the time, a lurking animosity in the way they responded to humans, as if they put considerable effort into their balky tendencies. Sometimes they seemed determined to be ornery, to make life frustrating. More often than not, they succeeded.

I spent more than one exhausting afternoon rounding up adventurous cattle that had breached some section of fence and wandered off on an expedition down the road or contentedly spread devastation through succulent fields of winter wheat. They proved extremely adept at getting on the wrong side of barbed wire, but utterly incapable of making it back to the main herd. Once I got behind them, hazing them toward the open gate that led where they clearly wanted to go, they'd often stampede off in any direction but the correct one, expressing their innate assumption that anywhere I'd want to take them would lead to pain and hardship.

Some individuals seemed to take offense at being imprisoned and pushed through fences as if it amounted to a matter of principal, no matter what lay on the far side. Even when I tried to ease their existence in some way—leading a herd to the water source in a new pasture, say, or administering a shot of red medicine to a steer with shipping sickness, the animals stubbornly resisted.

I learned from the start of the job that problems that arose in the course of daily ranch work were mine alone to handle. There are lots of things that are only a momentary inconvenience if someone else is around to help, but that consume half a day and all your patience and energy if you are on your own. Take, for instance, getting a vehicle extricated from a wet field or sandy draw. Or wrestling with a heavy, broken tractor part. Even in the little things—like closing gates, fixing fence, or feeding hay to livestock—another body more than doubles your rate of efficiency. And in those dilemmas where two people are as helpless as one, at least you gain a partner in misery.

Facing adversity without backup exercises one's powers of invention and creativity, no question about that. But, like most inventors, 90 percent of my strategies failed, and the 10 percent that succeeded were pretty lonely triumphs. After the nine failures that preceded success, I was usually bathed in sweat and decidedly pessimistic over the longevity of my victory.

I might have been thinking all of this while I faced off in the corral with the seven-hundred-pound heifer with bloat, but I had already reached the bathed-in-sweat stage. Worse yet, I hadn't even implemented the really tricky part of the job. I was stuck at step one, trying to herd the recalcitrant cow through a gate to a smaller pen. We looked at each other across the muddy, manure-studded enclosure. Sweat trickled into my eyes. The heifer had that obdurate stance animals assume when they've become convinced that whatever you have in mind for them is not in their best interest, and they're damned if they're going to cooperate. Over the last thirty minutes she'd proven a good deal more nimble than I, despite her grotesquely inflated belly. She was blowing hard, standing spraddle-legged next to the water tank, but looked entirely willing to continue battle and more than equal to the contest.

This heifer had a rebellious streak to begin with, enough so that I had learned to recognize her. Over the months after the herd arrived, she and I had met many times, usually on the wrong side of a fenced pasture. She was a fence-tester of the highest order, and her pathetic state stemmed from that bad habit. She'd decided that a field of green alfalfa looked more inviting than the dry rangeland where she'd been searching for forage along with the rest of the herd. She'd managed to wriggle through the strands of barbed wire and gorge herself on alfalfa for the better part of a morning before I'd discovered her.

At certain growth stages, alfalfa plants release gases that obstruct a cow's digestion. My patient had trespassed and gorged on the wrong side of the fence at the wrong time of year, and bloat was the result. Bloat is the rancher's colloquial term. Once you've seen it, you couldn't call it anything else. Well, this heifer deserved a dose of the disease, in my estimation, but her case wouldn't go away. Sometimes a cow will work things out over time, so to speak, but she'd apparently fed too long and gotten herself pretty efficiently blocked up. When several days passed and the only development was a bigger and rounder belly, the problem became mine as well as the heifer's. I'd been advised it was time to take some action. It turned out that a severe case of the bloat could actually be fatal.

Action in this case amounted to administering "about a Coke bottle's worth" of castor oil orally to lubricate the natural processes. If that failed, it would be the vet's turn to step in, but this first home remedy was mine to carry out. I'd noticed that Norman hadn't even hinted that he might be available to help.

I worked over the problem mentally a good while before starting to work. Coming up with a plan to subdue seven-hundred rebellious pounds equipped with four thrashing legs and then force the ingestion of a bottle of oil strained the limits of my imagination. On the other hand, scenarios featuring pain and humiliation were all too easy to conjure up.

The plan I settled on required me to herd the bloated victim into a smaller pen and then a blocked-off loading chute, which would close behind her. (An immobilizing squeeze chute would have been just the thing, but I didn't have one.)

Then, like a bronc-busting rodeo rider, I would straddle the sides of the fenced aisle and slowly work into a position hovering above the cow's neck. Straightforward so far.

I'd been told that if you could grab hold of a cow's tongue and pull on it, the animal would be utterly immobilized. Better yet, with tongue extended, the heifer would have little choice but to swallow the oil forced down her gullet. Accepting this as fact required a lengthy leap of faith, especially considering the potential for danger and comedy I was exposing myself to.

All of this assumed my ability to wrangle the heifer into position, an assumption still very much in doubt. Any sympathy I'd managed to work up toward the beast had evaporated in the sweat and frustration of my exertions. The solution to our standoff evolved when my patient noticed a new look in my eye. The fact that I picked up a two-by-four board and advanced toward her, brandishing it like a baseball player approaching the plate, no doubt helped my cause. With a mud-flinging final kick of her hind legs, she bolted into the small pen and eyed me suspiciously as I locked us into the confined space.

Over the course of another hour, I worked the rotund patient into the wooden chute, restrained her forward, backward, and upward motion by inserting boards closely around her, and had myself in position, bottle of oil at hand, preparing to wrestle with her slippery tongue.

Imagine trying to grab hold of a muscular, eight-inch garden slug that is really making an effort to get away. Add significantly more than a quarter ton of writhing body and a head hard as a sledge-hammer flailing around, and you might have a sense of the situation. It's hard to describe exactly how I got about half the bottle of castor oil into that heifer. I remember in separate images my legs scissor-locked around her neck, a slobbery cow tongue elusive as a big fish, the heifer's strangled protestations as I pried the bottle through her teeth and sloshed some of its slick contents down her throat.

Unlike many first-line remedies, this one actually worked. For several days it wasn't a good idea to be down-wind or too close to the deflating heifer, but at least I was absolved of further medical procedures.

— —

Meat machines. A crop with feet. I never grew fond of cattle. We regarded each other carefully, cognizant of our mutual dependence but suspicious and adversarial.

I suspect that my mixed feelings about cows were explained in part by latent pangs of guilt. Cows do not lead an enviable existence and my work made me an accomplice to their discomfort and eventual slaughter. Like a prison guard, I had to harden myself to my occupation. I suppose the resistant behavioral streak I noticed in cattle might be traced to their residual intuitive understanding of their fate.

From shortly after birth, cattle are harried inexplicably from place to place by shouting men on horseback or in pickup trucks; loaded onto crowded trucks like victims on the way to concentration camps; sold at auctions; penned in unvegetated feedlots where they're injected with growth hormones, steroids, and antibiotics.

Most young bulls are castrated with pocket knives. All cattle have their flesh seared with red-hot irons. Throughout life they are prone to the strange and deforming diseases I'd seen—ski toe, pink eye, and alfalfa bloat—any one of which might be cause for early termination. I remembered the mature cows judged not fertile enough that were shunted off to be dispatched.

During the less traumatic periods of life, cattle are released to fend for themselves, ranging across overgrazed land in search of food, withstanding the trials of heat and wind and blizzard without shelter, unwittingly cooperating in the process of fattening up.

Once they reach the apex of health, having endured a lifetime of trauma, cattle are summarily led off to slaughter, after which we consume the beasts we've groomed for that end. Small wonder I harbored a guilty twinge or two. Small wonder, too, that the animals rebelled in the few ways open to them.

Cattle are not known for their individualistic tendencies. If one is consistently off alone, away from the herd, it usually means something's wrong. Persistent stragglers are often sick or injured and can't keep up with the herd's movements. If I identified a sick animal quickly, a shot or two of medicine or a rest in the barn normally took care of the problem.

Just once I missed a stricken steer until it was too far gone to make a recovery. By the time I saw it, lying down at a distance from the other animals, it had abandoned any attempt to keep up. Over the course of several days I administered shots and brought it water. At one point, the yearling managed to struggle upright and plod over to the other animals. I hoped that signaled improvement, but the effort exhausted the steer, and it made no further recovery.

Each day I stood over the prostrate animal and listened to its shallow labored breathing, looked at the filmy eyes, finally realizing that it would inevitably die. Some of the healthy cattle stayed nearby, as if they made a point of keeping watch.

Another day passed and the steer still breathed. I should end this misery, I told myself. If I'd had a rifle I'd have shot it then, quick and merciful. Another day passed and the steer hung on. I had thought about how to kill it. The fastest and most efficient method I could imagine, given the tools at hand, was with a solid whack to the skull with a five-pound hammer. But I recoiled at the prospect. Firing a bullet into a dying animal's head, the result of an instant of pressure with my trigger finger, was one thing. Bludgeoning an animal to death with a hammer was another.

Once the necessity of killing the steer became obvious, I couldn't not follow through. The animal's tortured struggle for breath served as a testimony to my failure to see its weakness early enough. The least I could do was bring the prolonged and meaningless suffering to an end. *It's just a cow,* I thought.

I drove out to the pasture and again stood over the animal, hammer dangling from my gloved hand. Cattle grouped around me in the open field, watching silently. It was a moment when the vastness of the plains impressed itself upon me, as if I were in a white spotlight on an endless stage.

The steer didn't move. Its chest rose slightly with each breath. I yelled at the circle of cattle and waved my arms, but they just backed off a step. I read accusation in their dumb curiosity.

Finally I wielded the hammer. Taking aim, I brought the heavy tool down on the steer's skull. A dull thunk. Not hard enough. The steer shuddered and opened its eyes, but still breathed. Dammit, I muttered. I struck again, a sharper sound of concussion, and again, to be sure. Repetition numbed me in some way. My breathing got heavy, not from exertion but from emotion. Gorge rose in my throat. The rest of the herd had moved in closer. I felt their pressure. The steer lay as before, but now utterly still.

— —

Dead cattle, unless their numbers are great, are left to decompose on the dry land. But I felt a need to remove the evidence of death, and even more, to escape the condemning ring of cattle. I tied the steer's hind legs to the trailer hitch and almost ran to the cab. The dead animal dragged behind the truck like a weighted sack, making a wide furrow in the dirt. The live cattle trotted after the pickup in a trail of dust. They watched as I stopped at the brink of a sand wash and tipped the steer over the edge.

Without looking back, I drove off toward the distant white ranch house.

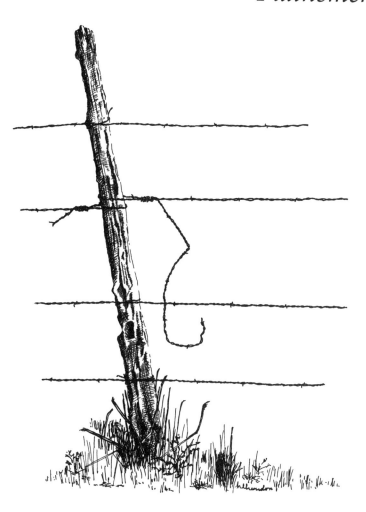

Plainsmen

I came to know Don because Norman periodically hired him to help with branding, herding, or other large jobs. Of the drifting, homeless, familyless workmen I had had a chance to meet, Don was the one I knew best.

One afternoon Don and I branded a small group of steers that had been missed before being shipped to the ranch. In the corner of a side corral we kindled a fire out of discarded barn wood and other scraps, heating the irons in the flames. The steers were too big for us to tackle, so Don would mount his horse and drop a neat loop of rope on the ground to catch the hind leg of each victim.

In the confined space there was little actual chase, more a lazy, half-speed surge of motion—horse pivots, rope swirls, the sudden collapse of steer hitting the ground. Then Don would drag the captured Hereford to the edge of the fire. We had trouble keeping the irons hot, had to keep hunting up more scraps of rotten lumber. The operation seemed bush league, like so many of the jobs I'd been involved in at the Steiger place.

Don moved stiffly, but never got behind on the task. When we took breaks, he shook a cigarette out of the pack in his shirt pocket, inhaled smoke deeply, tilted his hat back on his head. He shied away from conversation, as if ever preoccupied with thoughts.

Earlier, in the fall, we had spent another day together bucking hay bales onto a flatbed truck that idled down aisles in a large field. Don wore leather chaps, handled hay hooks as if they were second hands, hardly broke a sweat heaving the heavy cubes around. I muscled bales about, out of breath, barely keeping up with the truck; he moved with economy and precision. I ended that day as tired as I'd remembered being in years. Don gave me a small, shy grin as we walked off the field, flicked my arm lightly with his gloves, like an older brother after a tough Little League game.

In the evenings, after three or four beers, he revealed some of his past—a broken marriage that left bitter and unhealed wounds; a failed attempt at farming that ended with a bank auction; years of caretaking, riding the borders of another man's land; outside work that had left him with few friends, no possessions, short on security and resentful of women. He had gotten too old at forty something to still be shifting from job to job, and he knew it. I often caught sight of him at moments of rest standing with his hat cradled in both large hands, staring into the middle distance.

Without the lubrication of alcohol, he spoke hardly at all. Around me he acted courteously, with a polite restraint and a generous nature. When he spoke with Norman or ordered food at a cafe, he was polite to the point of caricature. But I sensed a deep well of anger at times, a streak of venom in his voice or an unguarded glance he shot at someone.

He told me this story. One winter he'd taken a job caretaking cattle on a ranch east of Pueblo, living there alone.

He went out on a midwinter morning to rope and brand several steers, pulling the horse trailer out close to the herd and unloading there. The first two animals gave him little trouble, but the third steer frustrated his roping attempts.

He gave determined chase, horse running flat out, lasso circling in wide arcs above his head, steer sprinting, feinting off at sharp angles. At the most focused moment of concentration, his galloping horse breathing over the escaping steer's rump, Don released his lasso. Just then, the horse streaked under a metal guy wire stretched out from a telephone pole. The cable struck in a diagonal line across Don's chest, snapping him out of the saddle. For twenty yards the running horse dragged him through sagebrush and cactus, until his foot worked loose from the stirrup.

He didn't know how long he lay unconscious in the isolated field, only that it was a long time and that after he woke he couldn't move. He lay with his eyes open, testing movement gingerly with different limbs, enduring excruciating pain.

As he related the story, Don turned a bottle of beer slowly around between his big calloused hands. Except for quick glances to check whether I was still listening he kept his eyes on the table. He seemed uncomfortable talking so long, but I encouraged him by meeting his eyes and making appropriate comments when he paused.

Over a period of several hours, he managed to roll to his belly and drag himself slowly across the ground, using the toes of his boots and his elbows. Gnarly sagebrush and clumps of prickly pear required painful detours. He stopped many times to rest, the pain numbing him. He remembered slipping into a half-conscious stupor while watching a beetle slowly pass in front of his face. But he finally regained his vehicle.

He pulled himself up to the running board, then grabbed the door handle, and eventually worked himself into the cab, where he slumped over the steering wheel. In time, he managed to start the truck, drive at a creeping pace across the rough pasture, and reach the highway. When he arrived at the emergency entrance to the Pueblo hospital he leaned on the horn until someone came out to get him. He had broken eight ribs and suffered internal bleeding. Since that day, he coped with chronic back pain. Whenever he bent over to clean a horse's hoof, he had to shuffle, doubled over, to a wall in order to lever himself upright. Don had a habit of hanging by his arms from a rafter or a door to relieve the pressure in his spine.

Because of my position, nearly all the people I met were men—laborers like Don or Steve, long-term foremen with families who ran ranches, the people who came to the Steiger place to buy hay, well-drillers, pump salesmen, combine crews. They were inheritors of a western legacy with roots going back to mountain men, sod-busters, wagon train drovers, cattle rustlers, the actors who had formed the frontier myths. Infrequent contact with women reinforced my impression of the High Plains as a male territory.

To the extent that generalizations are worth anything, the men were hard-working, resourceful by necessity, handy with animals and machinery, parochial in viewpoint, advocates of common sense, resentful of authority, and possessed by a tendency toward shyness.

The modern cowboy that Don represented can perhaps stake the most reasonable claim to carrying on the old western mythology. They typically own nothing beyond what is contained in their pickup truck and horse trailer. A man and a horse, a vehicle, a saddle and tack, a suitcase of clothing. The common round for these men consists of traveling from job to job, taking care of ranches, working with cattle, a different place every year, perhaps every season. Many ride the rodeo circuit some portion of the year to pick up extra cash. They work hard, drink hard, move often, and every one I met exuded what I can only describe as sadness.

The historic tradition embellished in the books I read as an adolescent presents a larger-than-life image of nineteenth-century western men—cavalry scout, Oregon Trail guide, dauntless explorer, cowboy. The characters I revered in books were men with keen eyes and steel nerves who traveled successfully through dangerous and harsh land, interpreting faint signs to stay alive. They defended themselves as much by their wits as with guns and knives. They generally were social outcasts by choice or necessity.

Just as the present-day cowboy image represented by Willie Nelson songs and beer commercials has no connection at all to people like Don, the legends of the Old West cling only lightly to fact. Hindsight and literary license award these frontier actors attributes of individuality, toughness, and rugged panache. Kit Carson, Wild Bill Hickok, Buffalo Bill Cody, Jim Bridger—legends that for good or ill, accurately or not, form the foundation of western myth.

The bulk of twentieth-century plains people has settled, and by doing so, has departed from the old nomadic life. Although the first settlers evolved out of the eras of exploration and early exploitation, even they had only fleeting connections to the old lore. Yet, in unspoken and insidious fashion, the legacy of freedom and hardship that characterizes western romantic tradition infuses the social underpinnings and expectations of the modern rural West.

Pete Hahn was one of my nearest neighbors, about ten back road miles from me. The phone book listed his ranch as being south of Rush. Pete retained a stubborn German accent and a clumsiness with English, despite being a second generation American. He'd inherited his small farm, house, and some equipment from his parents, had lived all his life within a ten-mile radius of his land, and had traveled out of eastern Colorado only once or twice in fifty years. Linguistic awkwardness symbolized his limited world view.

He was a quiet man, small in build, always a day late shaving, with a habit of looking away after meeting your gaze. I first spoke with him when he came over to buy a ton of hay and I coaxed him in for coffee.

"You married?" he asked.

I shook my head while pouring coffee, noticed the weathered look of Pete's hands around the cup, the dirt-lined cracks of skin.

"That's good," he continued. "Before I married I got no problems. Now I'm married, lots of things. All the time."

Pete was one of the few visitors who appeared to enjoy talking at my kitchen table. I pried memories of the old days out of him—descriptions of the first gasoline tractor on his place, for instance, a thing he still spoke of with a hint of childhood awe. I'd ask his advice on tending cattle with pink eye or the best way to train a herd to respect electric fence. He never made me feel foolish or ignorant. He'd throw in stories about his own ineptitude at ranching, a trait I never witnessed.

He married late, in his forties, and had a boy and a girl that were both under ten. After I'd come to know him better, Pete invited me to supper one evening. The way he acted around his family made me realize that his banter about marital problems must have been his way of generating conversation with a bachelor.

He had the air of a man who had withstood decades of loneliness and knew exactly what he had found. When he spoke to his children, even in reminding them to tend their chores, his voice was laden with gentleness. His glances, taking in the family, were visual caresses. I watched him savor his son's show of manliness when he took a turn steering the tractor through a field.

Pete's wife mirrored his reticence with speech, but had an air of cheerfulness and contentment about her. She rarely interjected herself into the conversation, but remained attentive as she competently served the meal. After eating that night, we played Monopoly with the children, and Pete manipulated his moves to benefit the kids, laughing with sheepish enjoyment when they pounced on him.

His children had picked up none of Pete's heavy accent. I wondered if his son would have any interest in staying on the place. Without saying so, Pete acted out his wish to pass on bits of knowledge, to turn his life and experience into a legacy his son could continue. Would I as a youngster—learning about life, getting hints of what lay outside of rural Colorado, feeling the peer pressure of friends leaving for exciting places—have been willing to stay on a little farm? I didn't envy Pete the potential for disappointment, nor his son the excruciating choice.

The family attended church twice a week: Wednesday night Bible class and Sunday service. Bibles and school books were the only reading material in the house, and the television had its viewing hours restricted.

Pete's operation stood in stark juxtaposition to the Steiger ranch. Everything about my place had the feel of temporary bivouac, an absentee landlord. The buildings slowly decayed because no one lived there. When we needed the use of a corral, a barn stall, a pasture, we cobbled together the boards or strung a line of fence. Norman ran things by telephone, visited infrequently, flew overhead in his Cessna to check out things aerially on his way somewhere else. I don't know in fact whether the ranch was simply a tax write-off, subordinate to other business interests like the water company, but it operated as if it were. Without care. Several times while I lived there the electricity was shut off because Norman didn't pay the bill. I camped out in the house and sometimes thought of the old building as nothing more than an oversized phone booth.

Pete's place, on the other hand, breathed familiarity in the shade trees that overarched the house, the smells in the kitchen, the daily chores his kids performed, the pet livestock that, despite their destiny, were spoken of with affection and intimacy. The buildings were old, but maintained scrupulously. Every stall in the barn was tight and latched shut with an easy click; every board in the corral was nailed snugly in place.

Pete knew his livestock individually. Not just the few horses but the range cattle, too. He knew which were prone to sickness, which had trouble calving. He pointed out one cow that had nearly died from a prolapsed uterus. When we drove his fields in a battered pickup, he observed the land with the intimate knowledge of one who had dug every post hole.

Pete would come to help me with some ranch project or problem, and, with a simple ease that left me gaping, he'd accomplish things that I had been sweating and cursing over. He had attained, through his lifetime of experience, an athlete's grace around ranch work.

Yet he exposed his parochial limitations with his stilted speech, his limited world view, his lack of comprehension over global events. One day he told me about his brother-in-law, who worked as a butcher in one of the large grocery store chains. "They pay him eight dollars an hour," he said, incredulously. "No man is worth eight dollars an hour!"

Pete's hourly wage, had he figured it, would have been ludicrously scanty. He owned his place outright and cut corners by using antiquated equipment, secondhand cars, an ancient tractor. He stood vulnerable to financial hardship nonetheless.

Late in the winter, during a warm spell, he asked if I'd come over to help him with calving. I didn't think he really required my assistance, but he knew from our conversations that I would enjoy being in on the births. His invitation was one of the few gestures of neighborliness that I received on the eastern plains. We sat on a pair of overturned buckets in a pool of warm sunlight. A cat rubbed against my legs. I watched a rooster work through the dirt barnyard, pecking with quick jerks at the ground. While we talked, Pete kept an eye on a cow that was in labor in the pen closest to us.

He had been getting up every three hours during the night over the last week to check on pregnant cows in the barn. His eyes were bloodshot with fatigue. Birthing difficulties were pretty rare, but regular enough to warrant close attention, especially when each animal represented a significant percentage of the herd. Problem deliveries, a prolapsed uterus, backward presentation, all could threaten the lives of cow and calf.

"Some big ranches just let the cows calve on the range," Pete told me. "If they have trouble, nobody comes to help. Lots more die that way."

The warm day made us sleepy. We went long periods without talking, bathing in the springlike weather. The cow breathed heavily and moved with obvious discomfort. She couldn't find a good position, and alternated between lying on her bulging side or standing with her legs wide apart, sides heaving. This went on a long time.

"She's starting," Pete suddenly pointed. "See the front feet?"

The cow was obviously pushing, straining, her neck stretched out, eyes almost closed. Absurdly, I expected to see her sweating. We could see the pearl-colored hooves barely appearing, tiny and perfect and unbelievably clean.

"It looks good," Pete said. "We just wait."

Proper position for birth is front feet first, followed by the head—a pose like a diver's, arms pointed out, head tucked down between them. The calf looked to be in good form, but the cow couldn't seem to push it out—just those dainty front feet pointing the way, but nothing more.

Finally Pete stood up, brushed his hands on his jeans. "We need to help." He picked up a length of broomstick and some twine. I followed to the pen.

Our presence made the cow nervous, distracted her from the labor. She wouldn't let us behind her, but Pete murmured to her consolingly as he worked his way down her flank and looped twine around the hooves of the calf. He tied the other end to the middle of the broom handle and told me to get on one side.

"Don't pull hard," he said, taking up position. "Just help her."

The cow circled the pen, agitated, towing us behind like barnyard water-skiers. Pete clucked and reassured her, but the cow had forgotten about giving birth.

"Pull a little." Pete and I leaned back.

More of the legs, and then the pink calf nose appeared. The cow stopped walking, feeling the movement, and pushed. Most of the head squeezed out. We pulled to help. The shoulders stuck and then eased past. I heard the cow moan, an elemental sound. Suddenly the calf slithered out in a wet, slippery clump and plopped to the ground.

Pete leapt to the newborn's face and peeled away mucous and bits of membrane from its mouth and nostrils. The cow moved away after a quick sniff, as if disowning involvement. Pete was on his knees in the mud and manure. He blew in the calf's face, this new, nearly alive thing. The little animal started and took a breath, initiating life. Grabbing the slimy mucous, Pete went to the cow and rubbed it on her face, giving her the scent of her baby.

"Her first one," he said, coming back to the calf. "Sometimes they won't take them."

He helped the calf to a wobbly stand, looked over the pristine color of the little animal, never again to be as clean. He picked the baby up and took it to the mother, held it for her to sniff, laid it next to her. The cow took no interest in the life she'd just produced.

We left them together and retreated to watch. For a long time the exhausted cow just stood dumbly, ignoring her newborn on the ground. The calf lay there, helpless, mute, curled up. The mother walked around the pen and stood some distance away. Pete and I waited, our hands still slimy.

Eventually the cow nosed over to her baby, as if investigating a tuft of grass she might eat, and smelled the small body, her big nostrils flaring. Then, her large coarse tongue lapped the calf's face, came out again, began cleaning the baby with rough caresses.

Pete let his breath out and I realized I'd been holding mine too. "Good. She took it." He looked down at his hands and we went to the faucet to wash.

— —

Pete and Don represented two threads of the loosely woven human web that is High Plains society. Through shared time and confidences, I came to consider these two men as friends. I touched superficially some others—the regulars at the cafe on doughnut day, the reserved men who sat at my kitchen table, the crew on the ranch near Lamar. At times I considered myself an invisible observer. Although I wrestled with cattle or stood with men drinking coffee, I wasn't swallowed up in the life the same way they were.

Plainsmen

It was as if I explored an entirely foreign medium, observing, feeling new sensations, knowing all along that eventually I'd return to the other plane of existence where I belonged. I felt that I left no impression where I went, no lasting mark, but that the people, the land, the gulf of space, imprinted themselves upon me.

Once in a while I read a thin rural newspaper called *The Ranchland News.* It covered a disproportionate patch of geography on a par with the small phone book, threw a thin net across the far-flung human catch. I cared little about the usual rural grist—crop predictions, feeder sales, drought forecasts—news I overheard at the cafe anyway. I went right for the social column, both for comic value and out of simple curiosity.

> *Vern and Wilma Kruger took a shopping trip to Colorado Springs last Tuesday. They got all their supplies and said they had a real good lunch at the Best Western Hotel.*
>
> *Velma Hodgekins, Carla May, Fiona Babcock, and Fay Whitstone had their usual bridge club meeting last Friday. Velma brought her home-baked apple pie.*
>
> *Robert Bidwell, 12, son of Roy and Martha Bidwell of Yoder, won the regional spelling bee contest for*

eastern Colorado and will go to the state finals next month. His family looks forward to traveling with him to Glenwood Springs for the event.

For people, even neighbors, who might not meet for months on end, the news provided a way to connect. Most of the time they were too busy, spaced too widely, or too in need of a quiet rest to seek company.

A good deal of rural socializing happens at chance meetings on a sidewalk in front of a bank, between the cabs of two trucks idling next to each other on a deserted road, at an auction when two ranchers bid against each other, outside of church on Sunday.

Besides the logistical obstacles to social life where distances are great and work all-consuming, there is something else inhibiting interaction—something taciturn and stubbornly lonely in the way people go about their lives. Plains people don't frequently invite each other over for dinner or cocktail hour.

As the months of winter progressed I became more intuitively aware of the pulse of the plains. At night I'd sometimes wander through the dark silence under the crisp sharp stars. I sensed the livestock in the fenced enclosures, biding their time, loosely held prisoners. I listened for the surreptitious movements of deer and coyote, owl and lark, playing out the intense but hidden drama of prey and predator, raising young, seeking cover, moving along pathways I only dimly perceived, sensitive in ways I would never match.

And I heard in some faint way the human heartbeats thudding along with mine, keeping time across the endless space, as the earth sped through night.

High Plains Blizzard

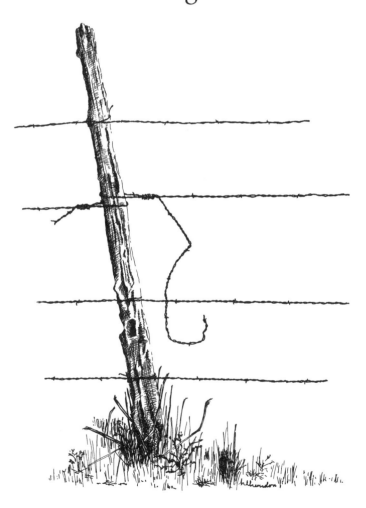

High Plains Blizzard

W ind is the salient climatic feature on the High Plains.
People who live in that semi-arid, flat, spacious environment unconsciously bear themselves along at a slight tilt,
as if pushing against something. Usually they are, because
they're resisting the almost ceaseless and unimpeded flow of
air. On a rare calm day, the lack of wind is, peculiarly, a
presence by its very absence. Plains folks straighten up from
their forward lean, relax their confrontational tight expres-
sions, breathe deeply, and glance about warily for the miss-
ing foe.

I had become intimate with the caresses and pum-
melings of moving air. My house stood out like a topographic
knob. When I worked outside I felt the wind work at eroding
me, picking at me as if I were a hunk of soft rock.

Wind had lifted and moved the topsoil in smudgy
clouds behind the tractor when I planted winter wheat in late
summer. When snow fell, storm gales plastered the flakes to
the windward side of the ranch buildings and deposited
white dunes leeward. Drifting tumbleweed, desiccated flot-
sam, rested briefly in protected road ditches or behind cattle
pens. Even inside the white ranch house I heard air moaning
in the exhaust stack of the propane heater and would wake up
in the night to the bony scrabbling-finger sounds of cottonwood branches against window panes.

On the morning of March 10th wind of unusual
strength streamed down across the land from the north, an

invisible airy ocean rushing up a tidal bore. From the window above the kitchen sink I watched the cottonwood branches flailing like wild arms, trees cowering under the attack; saw an old dried-up maize stalk fly by at eye level. When I ventured out past the protective corner of house, airborne grit and topsoil abraded my exposed face like fine-grained sandpaper. Tumbleweed hopped and skittered and cart-wheeled through the fields as if alive.

The thirteen hundred head of young range cattle grouped together nervously, trotted in a long jouncing lap around the fenced periphery of the pasture. I drove the ranch truck around the same route checking on the Herefords. Tumbleweed was trapped in thick, weighty layers against the fence, actually working metal staples loose and ripping electrical wire from its attachments.

I fought shorts in the charged strands and nailed up wire for hours, until the futility of the battle forced my surrender. The massed weight of tumbleweed pressing along the fence felt like the scary heft of a horse leaning against you when you're bent over cleaning its hoof. Gusts of wind alternately wrenched the truck door from my grasp or powerfully resisted my attempts to close it.

The cattle weren't testing the viability of boundaries in any case. They bunched up behind whatever shelter they could find, in sandy washes and against the southern border, their blunt backsides turned to the wind, hair pressed into flat whorls, their bleating and lowing sounds snatched away in the gale.

Pikes Peak hunkered impassively under a boiling black anvil of cloud to the west. The storm hadn't been forecast, but the approach of frightening weather telegraphed its arrival in the brutal line of sky, the extraordinary wind, the scent of dirt in the air, the wall-eyed looks cattle gave me as I drove past.

It had been an easy winter for people and livestock, but it had been hard on the land. Almost no rain or snow had fallen in months. What little moisture trickled from the sky had dried up in a matter of a day or two. Winter wheat had received no protective snow cover. Wind chiseled away at the plant roots. The green shoots looked dusty and stunted, wind-chapped and dry. I had been able to drive the truck through the fields all season without fear of getting stuck.

The local talk all centered on the hope for spring rain. Without it the crops would struggle. Watching men talk, even from a distance, I could read the concerned shake of heads, the scanning looks over the horizon, and know that their words were about water.

It looked like winter's accumulated energy would spend itself in one horrendous, unpredicted storm, arriving just as High Plains farmers were gearing up for spring.

— —

Responding to my own herd inclinations, I abandoned my usual solitary lunch habit to drive into Rush, eight miles distant. The attacking weather nudged me instinctively to seek the solidarity of humans. No matter that I had little chance of meeting someone I knew, I savored the prospect of exclaiming at events in the company of neighbors, all of us participants in a drama, bunched up in the cafe in much the same manner as the bewildered young cattle on the open range.

I never made it. Six miles along the dirt road the ancient, much abused farm truck gave out a startling series of loud clanks and stopped abruptly. The engine was still capable of roaring with uninhibited power, but a terminal failure in the drive train rendered that horsepower useless.

A few minutes of tinkering under the chassis exhausted my mechanical resources. The howling wind made me desperate to do something, to escape. I struggled to get the truck door closed and started walking the six miles back home. Soon my windward hip began to ache from the strain of the pronounced lean I had to maintain. I looked back at the truck, thought about holing up in the cab, but then plunged on.

The air flowed as steadily and powerfully as a massive river current, and it carried atmospheric flood wreckage with it. I had become inured to dust and soil in the air, but this wind picked up small gravel, minute shrapnel that stung my face painfully. Clumps of hay, strands of vegetation, and tumbleweed flowed past or skipped across the road at a furious speed. Severed barbed wire lay on the ground, ripped from fence posts and flung aside.

At one point I realized that it had never entered my mind to walk the shorter distance to the cafe, where I could have presumably bummed a ride. My need at the time had been to get immediately home. The truck had imbued me with a feeling of invulnerability, provided me with shelter from the elements, the ability to flee, but that security had been plucked away. Responding to the lure of the ranch house, the nest I'd made there, I unhesitatingly chose the longer, riskier walk.

I tried walking backward to relieve hip pain and expose my other side to the wind-driven battering. Too slow. An insistent urge to hurry, to beat whatever was coming, quickened my pace. Breathing became more difficult, as if the maelstrom sucked my lungs dry, a sort of drowning. No one drove the roads. I passed familiar landmarks—the old farmstead that meant I had four miles to go, the dirt crossroads two miles from home.

The storm's front edge wore away at me as I walked. The exposed side of my face was numb before I made it halfway home. The rush of wind became a roaring sound in my ears so overwhelming, so menacing, that I couldn't imagine it ever dying away.

— —

There was nothing I could do for the cattle on the range. Even if I could have rounded them all together and driven them through the wind, I had no sheltered place to put them. They would have to weather the storm on instinct and brute endurance. I had half a dozen head of fortunate sick cattle penned up in the barn along with the solitary ranch horse, an animal I had named after Norman.

The first pellets of snow were falling as I reached the house; hard, gritty flake nuclei that had survived long enough to reach the ground. Only midafternoon, but I had to turn on the lights to see. Black sky shut off the sun, and clouds of dust further darkened the horizon. Snow drove by the window in horizontal streaks, like tracks of light. I collapsed in the overstuffed chair and let the blare of roaring storm slowly diminish in my ears.

The phone rang, startling me. It was Norman. "Stay inside!" he cautioned. "There's something big coming."

"Right, Norm." If the house had suddenly caught fire I wouldn't have left it.

"You better collect some water and see if you can find candles in case the electricity goes," he added. "I'll try to keep calling."

High Plains Blizzard

I felt the house shudder under the heavy gale, heard wind shrieking in the propane stack, thought feebly about where I might go if the roof tore off. My nearest neighbor lived farther away than the six miles I'd just walked.

Snow had already worked its way under the back door in a small drift. The north side of the house was sheathed in an unbroken layer of white, compacted by wind. Out a side window I caught sight of a tiny sparrow that fluttered up out of a clump of weeds and was snatched from sight by the gale. It occurred to me that on my entire walk home, a stretch usually alive with horned larks, western meadowlark, hawks, falcons, jackrabbits, and coyote, I hadn't noticed a breath of life.

I ran the bathtub full of water, found old bottles and big pots to fill, rounded up a kerosene lamp and some candles that I set strategically around the house. The merciless beating of the storm distracted me from concentrating on anything else. For hours I paced the inside circumference along the walls, my fortifications, stopping at each window to watch the deadly snow whip past, my view of the familiar ranch yard cut to five feet.

Lying in bed that night I visualized my retreat to the dusty, cobwebbed, mouse-turd-sprinkled crawl space beneath the house. Gusts of wind rattled the windows and the wooden framework groaned and creaked ominously under the strain. I awoke again and again from a jumpy dreamless sleep, more and more certain that the ranch building wouldn't last, finally convinced that it was simply a matter of time before the roof sailed away and I would have to scurry beneath the foundation, burrowing like a plains animal.

I pictured my settlers on Little Horse Creek. The couple lay in bed, without speaking, listening to the storm tear and howl around their home, hearing the alarming crack of cottonwood branches. No electricity, no telephone, no running water in the house. One of them would move restlessly under the blankets, and they would reach for each other in the darkness.

In a way, the obvious vulnerability of the settlers would be a more realistic situation than my own. I had the illusion of security brought through telephone wires, but Norman could no more help me in a crisis than I could help the cattle. To be independent of electricity and running water, to be accustomed to reading the weather and reacting appropriately would have put me in a more self-reliant stance. And had I been in the settlers' situation, I would likely have had my livestock close at hand, under shelter.

By morning the storm seemed, if possible, to have intensified. The sounds of the blizzard made me cold by association, so that I pulled my chair right up against the constantly running heater, warmed my hands with mugs of coffee. Norman called in midmorning, surprised to get through at all.

"I'm stuck down here in Lamar," he shouted. "It's supposed to last another day." Even from inside his hotel room the wind made such an overwhelming impression on him that he fought it with his strident voice.

"The weather station down here measured wind speeds above one hundred miles an hour," he called. "Then the wind cups blew off the roof! Now they don't know how hard it's blowing."

Snow steadily buried the house. Hour by hour compacted drifts inched up the windows; dirty snow, laced with brown topsoil. I raised a window and poked my finger into the cold, hard entity that inexorably entombed the building, like a foundered ship with the tide rising over it.

My thoughts sheered away from the cattle. Nevertheless, I was haunted by pictures of scattered, shadowy animal shapes numbed by days of wind, matted with snow and ice, energy and warmth and the forces of life ebbing away in the effort to sustain themselves. No shelter, no food, no water, just endless howling wind and the stinging bullets of snow. The band of sick cattle under the barn roof entered my thoughts as well. They hadn't been fed in more than a day.

Twenty-four hours had buffered me from the memory of my walk, and I admitted to a certain curiosity about the storm. Each time the thought of venturing out presented itself, I beat it back with sensible arguments, but the perverse urge to be out in the weather, to experience the incredible elements, persisted.

I had read accounts of pioneers who, having lost their bearings in plains blizzards, and groping about in aimless circles, finally perished within yards of safety. Overcoming a twinge of melodramatic self-consciousness, I lashed stout clothesline rope around my waist and tied the other end to the porch railing. My sheepishness vanished once I'd shoveled through the thick drift that blocked the door and stepped outside.

Visibility, even with the wind at my back, extended to the end of my outstretched arm and no farther. I bumped face first into the white pump house without ever seeing it. Swirling snow and the torrent of air made me feel tossed about, upended, as if in frothing surf. I rechecked the knot at my waist, wondered if I'd tied the other end of the lifeline securely enough.

I glimpsed a titanic drift looming off to my right, rising in the lee of my house. Eventually I stumbled against the corral fence, a reassuring landmark, and grasped the top board firmly. Snow filled the corral nearly to the fence top. I labored to the barn, half swimming through the cloying drifts, and followed the rough wall to where a door should have been. I couldn't have come to the wrong side of the barn. . .

High Plains Blizzard

My mind had been slowed by the buffeting storm. I stood there dumbly, leaning against the rough boards, until it dawned on me that I was perched on snow that was deeper than the door was high. By the time I'd shoveled away enough drift to pry open the buried entrance and squeeze through, my drenched clothes were frozen stiff as wood. I left the rope dangling down the front of the snowdrift.

The cattle stood in a tight little group surrounded by piles of snow that had worked in through cracks in the building. I pitched them wads of hay off a bale and looked around for the horse. I'd left Norman in a sheltered, fenced-in lean-to attached to the barn. It was out of the wind there and the floor was dry—but the horse had disappeared. Then I noticed the hoof prints. They led me up the flank of a drift and over the buried fence where the storm obliterated any further tracks.

"What the hell?" I wondered out loud. The horse had wandered off into the teeth of a howling blizzard. Norman had borne a fair measure of verbal abuse on occasion, as the namesake of Norman the landowner, but the beast's inexplicable disappearance was a grave concern. It might have been within ten feet of me, but to search would be ridiculous.

Returning to the house, I struggled against the full weight and violence of the storm. Even with my eyes narrowed to slits, I couldn't lift my face to the wind. Step by floundering step I reeled myself in, coiling loops of line in my hand as I moved, praying the knot would hold. The effort made me gasp for air. I smelled dirt in the snow that drove against my face. Although the ranch house tugged solidly back at the end of my rope, the reality of a dry, warm, calm home close by seemed impossible, right up to the moment that I grasped the doorknob and fell inside.

"Jesus, Jesus, Jesus!" I panted. My icy clothes clattered when I moved, my face felt whipped red. I anchored myself firmly beside the heater, utterly cured of any desire to combat the tempest outside.

Day blended seamlessly into night. My sleep was again broken by abrupt jerks into wakefulness. For much of the night I listened, eyes open, to the tortured straining of a house withstanding an unfathomable beating.

Much later I drifted into deep sleep. When I woke, the world was dead calm, silent as a cave.

― ―

Where's the horse? I wondered, once the fact that the storm had ended penetrated my consciousness.

Open ground had been swept nearly bare by the wind, but anywhere an obstruction stood, snow drifts reflected the object's shape in elongated humps. Even tufts of grass owned tails of snow, white shadows. South of the house a drift stood twenty feet high and one hundred feet long, completely covering an old chicken shed and obliterating half the large corral.

I found Norman's hoof prints again. This time they wandered up and over the snow ridge that had formed behind the ranch house. The drift was so wind-hardened that the horse's hooves made only shallow impressions. I stood on top and surveyed the tattered landscape. Storm wreckage lay about as if a sudden truce had been called and everything had been dropped in midbattle—barbed wire, tumbleweed, vegetation torn up by the roots, scraps of trash blown in from some distant source.

I followed tracks down the far side, where they vanished into the edge of the drift. *Buried,* I thought. The horse had stood there out of the wind and had been buried alive. I began digging into the hard, gritty layers furiously with a grain scoop, expecting with each thrust to hit frozen horseflesh. Sweat trickled into my eyes. Already the day was warm, the sky an unbelievable blue, the snow a radiant blinding whiteness. The two-day blizzard seemed unimaginable. I dug a small room out of the drift, panting, almost tearful with inexplicable emotion. No horse.

I took an exploratory walk around the house to rest from the exertion and was met by an apparition in a bare spot in the front yard: Norman, coated with plates of ice like chain mail on a steed from Camelot. He pawed with his hoof and gave me a wild, spooky glance. His cold armor jangled.

We looked at each other, storm castaways taking stock. When I approached more closely, the horse shied and trotted off. I brought water and a bucket of feed and then backed away. Norman eyed me without any sign of recognition, and I left him to recover at his own pace.

All morning I wielded the shovel, scooping snow out from inside the north end of the house, tunneling a path from the back door to the driveway. My pickup truck had weathered the storm in a doorless ranch building. I could see only a corner of the bumper and one tail light under the drifted snow. Once I'd exhumed the vehicle, I lifted the hood. Snow was packed tightly around the engine as if meticulously injected to form a perfect white mold.

Norman phoned. "How're the fields?"

"Bare."

"Good. I'm flying the plane out there. Can't drive. All the roads are closed with drifts." He waited for me to say something, but nothing occurred to me.

"Sit tight. I'll bring you some food."

This was where I had it over my settlers. Nobody in a Cessna would have come to their aid with groceries from Safeway. How long would they have had to wait for some contact?

High Plains Blizzard

The field of winter wheat next to the house had been burned and torn by the wind. The plants that were left clung to ground that looked polished and blasted like sculpture, hard as kiln-fired pottery. The only places that had collected snow were the shallow washes and the fence line; otherwise, naked ground raked by wind, polished by sand and snow, punished by the elements.

After Norm's plane bounced to a stop, he climbed down slowly and stood on the blasted ground without saying anything, nudged a forlorn tuft of winter wheat with his boot.

"Very bad," he finally said. "There are dead cattle everywhere between here and Colorado Springs." He looked across the fields. "You wouldn't believe the size of the drifts across the highways. It'll take weeks before they're clear."

"I think I might believe them," I said.

We walked to the house; he carried a shopping bag of food. Norm studied the behemoth drift for a long moment and then looked at me. I thought I read the same quality of assessment in his eyes as the look I had given the horse, looking for clues to the storm's impact.

He made some phone calls and we toured the barn, meltwater already dripping from the eaves, making mud in the paddock. The bunch of cattle blinked in the sun's glare as they looked at us.

"We'd better fly around and see what it looks like," Norman sighed.

While the small plane banked and circled, zoomed low over the ground, the enormity of the storm became clear. Dead cattle were indeed everywhere, dotting the open fields, clumped in mass graves in the snow-choked washes, lying along fences. The live animals stood dumbly next to the dead, heads lowered as if waiting for the next blow.

Many animals had been driven south before the wind, walking over drifted fence lines. We spotted the Triangle brand on cattle six miles south of our land.

"I'll drop you off here," Norm shouted, his face grim. He banked sharply around. "You can start walking back, herding the live ones as you come."

Dead animals far outnumbered the living. The small band I began gathering up had the same numbed and crazy look in their eyes that the horse had had. Some abandoned dead companions only reluctantly and stubbornly circled around to return. I ran awkwardly after them, afraid to push too hard.

In every small wash, in every snowdrift, more cattle had perished. Each depression of land had offered a tenuous haven for the wind-harried beasts, but then was transformed into a deadly trap as snow collected and gradually buried them to a depth from which they couldn't escape. Finally, when the panicked and exhausted cattle gave up their struggle, the blanket of snow suffocated them. The dead cows' nostrils were packed with snow and dirt.

High Plains Blizzard

Some were buried but still alive. At each drift I stooped over the breathing holes and listened for labored sounds of life. Once in a while I heard breathing down the dark tubes, and dug and kicked my way through layers of hard snow until I encountered brown and white bodies, the live entwined with the dead.

One little steer I uncovered gave me crazed, white-eyed looks and struggled desperately to its feet, where it tottered forward a few steps before falling on its side, dead. A few others managed to recover themselves, rising out of white graves, visibly in shock. I thought of earthquake or avalanche victims pinned beneath rubble, waiting mutely for rescue while their life sap drained slowly off. I stood over a dying steer whose legs kept moving in a walking motion, scraping circles in the snow. I remembered making snow angels as a child.

For two days Norman and I crisscrossed the fields in search of live remnants of the herd with the Triangle brand. I encountered ranchers from the north looking for cattle driven onto our land. No one seemed to want to talk. People's mouths were tight lines. Warm weather, a cynical springlike aftermath to the storm, shriveled the drifts, exposing piles of cattle. I worked numbly at the tasks of recovery:

repairing fence, tending sick animals, uprighting sprinkler spans. In two days the work of months and years had been undone like toys crushed at the whim of a giant.

We lost eight hundred head out of thirteen hundred animals, a percentage on a par with neighboring ranches. The winter wheat crop was a complete loss. When I traveled the roads and went to small towns on errands, the topic on everyone's lips was the blizzard, the worst storm in fifty years. Pickup trucks idled on dirt roads, cab to cab, and ranchers shared their stories. After the initial shock passed, people seemed to find solidarity in talk.

A family not far away had lived out the scenario I had feared most, huddled together for a day in their basement after their roof zipped off in the wind like the lid of a tin can. I heard of an older couple who survived the storm stranded on a country road inside their car. National Guard helicopters airlifted food to farms cut off from town by monstrous snowdrifts. A neighbor's center pivot sprinkler had been picked up by the wind and wrapped around a telephone pole.

Within days, rendering-service trucks cruised the farm roads like circling vultures, picking up the thousands of dead animals with front-end loaders and carting the carcasses off to be ground into meal for chicken feed additive or something equally prosaic.

When I heard one of their trucks rattle into the yard and confronted a grizzled, bloodshot-eyed driver at the back door, I couldn't hide my disgust with his occupation, even though my reaction was unfair. I just pointed to the wash where the dead cattle lay and closed the door in his face.

In town, normal life quickly resumed. Ceiling drips dried up, streets were cleared, schools reopened. Papers sported storm headlines for a few evenings and then moved fitfully on to fresh topics.

But ranch work was never the same for me after the blizzard. It took weeks to regain a positive attitude toward the jobs of reconstruction, to emotionally accept the next season. And after the storm, I never again felt the same sense of satisfaction over a tight line of fence, a neatly grooved field, or a healthy bunch of well-tended cattle.

Recovery ... Transition

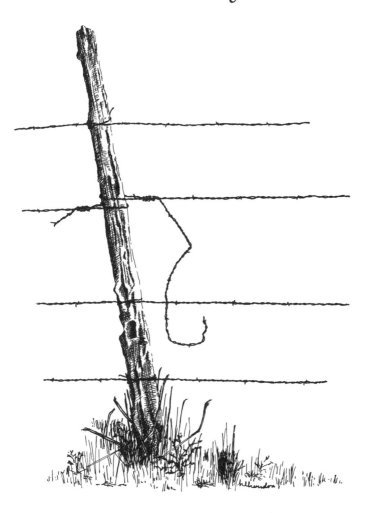

S pring began with the catastrophic storm, leaving carcasses and wind-burnt crops behind it. Early summer
continued the ruinous trend with a spate of dry, hot, windy
weather. A bit of timely rain would have gone a long way
toward aiding crop recovery, not to mention restoring human morale. Some hopeful green shoots, soil with enough
moisture to hold itself together, any small beneficence of nature would have helped bury memories and turn attention to
the future.

As it was, those with insurance collected crop and
livestock money that only partially restored an uneasy balance; those without sank further into debt. Most winter wheat
fields were plowed under and replanted with another crop
that languished anemically in the unrelenting drought.

I spent weeks propping up fence line, restringing
wire, tending to the bovine survivors of the blizzard. The storm
and the continuing meteorological harshness had sapped my
optimism, drained my resilience. I didn't own the place, yet the
futility, the required hard-headed stubbornness in the face of
failure knocked the supports from under my attitude.

What, in God's name, is the point? I'd think, up to my
elbows in tumbleweed in a road ditch, trying to find a strand
of barbed wire. *What are people doing, trying to water and raise
crops in this climate?*

I lacked the perspective and commitment of old-
timers, people who'd seen drought and blizzard before, people

who'd struggled through financial disaster time after time, people who had sunk their roots, their sweat, their savings, into squared-off parcels of land and, by God, had no choice but to outlast it again. My response was to get away from the futility and smell of loss.

Rain clouds rarely appeared in the sky, and nearly always missed the ranch even if they dropped a scattered pattering of moisture. More often, the clouds I watched were the dirt-dark, earthbound ones, choking fogs of blown topsoil. Clouds that eclipsed the sun.

Nothing so catastrophic as the dust bowl, but terrifying nonetheless. Terrifying to see what we have done with all our plowing and sifting and turning of the earth. Terrifying, too, in an obscene way, to watch the land be denuded, shamelessly left vulnerable, and then stripped layer by earthy layer.

Norman sent me east again to help rebuild a toppled section of sprinkler; it was like working on a monstrous tinker toy that had been carelessly wrecked in a fit of temper. Throughout the eastern half of the state, wind had drifted dirt into dunes against telephone poles and fence lines, desert dunes with spumes of fine topsoil curling from their peaks in the breeze, reminiscent of the snow piled by blizzard gales. I drove with my headlights on at midday. When I blew my nose black grit came out. My face turned gray even with the windows rolled up.

In the trailer where I stayed with the rest of the work crew, the air was as thick as if there had just been a fire in the oven. We ate sandwiches at noon with the lights on. The bread was full of dirt. The only comfort lay in getting free of the hounding, soil-laden wind. When one of the ranch pickups wouldn't start, we checked the engine and found the distributor cap full of soil as fine as dust. We worked in a cloud. When I looked down the sprinkler span, the other men were shadowy ghost figures in the maw of an awful dry storm, a storm that insidiously robbed the foundation from beneath our feet. Even close up we had to shout to each other.

Farmers applied for disaster relief. They abandoned crops and plowed with chisel attachments to turn up huge clods of earth too heavy, in theory, for the wind to carry off.

Ironically, and in contrast to the human distress, wildlife seemed unaffected by the hardship. Although I knew that the blizzard and drought must have exacted its toll, life that existed always on the fringe of human activity went on with little sign of stress or devastation.

While shoveling snow after the blizzard, I heard the unmistakable call of a killdeer. I noticed a pair of sparrow hawks nesting in a nearby cottonwood tree, intent and focused on each other, on their shared endeavor. Rough-legged hawks I'd watched all winter circled restlessly, sometimes in groups of four or five, as if awaiting some critical signal to depart; one by one they disappeared, flying toward the tundra of the Far North. Then, filling the vacuum created by their departure, Swainson's hawks arrived from South America, pulled north to spend another summer foraging across the plains, following tractors, watching attentively from fence posts.

A burrowing owl established itself in a warren of prairie dog burrows in the same rangeland occupied by our cattle. I watched it stand on long legs, bending and bowing, gesturing like a tidily attired professor lecturing on the attributes of earthen homes.

Sandhill cranes flew overhead, their ungainly size and huge wingspread overcome by balletlike grace. Even after dark I sometimes heard their burbling chuckly calls and could imagine their gray silhouettes, the quick upbeat of their flight, the wingtip to wingtip symmetry of the flock.

I heard coyote less often in the spring and early summer, and the mule deer congregated in smaller numbers at the cottonwood grove. I assumed that the quieter, more dispersed habits were the behavioral compromises demanded by raising young.

A crowd of blackbirds took up noisome residence in the shade trees around the house. Their droppings hit the ground like rain, and the racket they made, squawking and wheezing, became intolerable at times. I took to slamming out of the house and chucking rocks into the trees in a futile attempt to chase them off.

— —

Norman came out to find shelter in the relative peace of the ranch. He'd arrive unannounced, ostensibly to direct some project, but we'd end up sitting together in the cool quiet kitchen, plugging away at a pot of coffee. Those days, Norman had the look of a harried man who'd discovered the meaning of sanctuary.

His usual nervous energy had been siphoned off in some way by the blizzard. He kept up with things, but more out of habit than drive. I knew the financial blow must have been severe, but a malaise underlay his attitude. Even in my presence he sometimes brooded. He told me that he'd been lucky to have blizzard insurance through Lloyd's of London. The dead cattle weren't a total loss, but his hopes had been flattened. He planned to sell off the remainder of the herd as soon as prices looked advantageous.

Norman often lapsed into fantasies about rural living, the bliss of self-sufficiency. "All the wind out here," he'd sigh. "You could generate your electricity, pump water for the house, never have to pay utility bills." I felt incorporated into his schemes, as if he deviously tried to plant the same seeds in my imagination. "A person could do worse than to fix up a place like this."

One day he asked abruptly, "What're your plans?"

"I think I'll move on this summer." The finality in my voice startled me. I'd thought a good deal about getting to the next thing in life, about ending the self-imposed solitude, moving back on the main track; but the unequivocal assertion in my statement made me realize that my sentiments had hardened unconsciously.

"I like the place," I went on, softening my sudden statement. "The job's been a good one, but it isn't what I want from life. I need to be around people again."

"You need a woman!" Norm jumped in. "Fix up the house, run the ranch together, hang some curtains."

"I won't argue the woman part," I agreed. "But not here."

We got into Norm's car and meandered around the ranch, drove the wheel-track paths through the struggling fields, past the wary stares of cattle. Norm drove into Rush, switching off the car phone on the way.

"Wait here," he said when he parked outside the cafe. He returned with a six-pack of cold beer and set it between us. The sweaty bottles clanked against each other.

We parked on a county road, a view of plowed fields and fence line and skeletal sprinklers. The sun plunged slowly toward the mountains behind us, lengthening the vehicle's blocky shadow. We each held the neck of a beer bottle, savored drowning the dust in our throats. I opened my window and the warm, pungent presence of the plains filled the cab. A meadowlark blasted the quiet with melody at high volume. Wind rustled the weeds faintly, no more sound than a snake makes moving through dry grass.

"My grandfather started all this." Admiration blended in Norm's voice with resentment for what he'd inherited. "During the Depression he went to a banker in Kansas for a loan. Without money he would have gone belly-up. He told that banker he didn't know how he'd pay it back or exactly when, but that he'd be good for it."

Norm drank, looked hard at the bottle. I realized how young he was, how wealth and responsibility and the burdens of ambition separated us more significantly than years.

"They shook hands on the deal and that was his start, what got him over the hump. A couple-thousand-dollar loan on a handshake made the difference."

When we drove back, we went slowly, the way old men drive their clattering farm trucks. Norm dropped the empty bottles out the window into a trash can at Rush. The sun hovered on a ridge near Pikes Peak, hot orange through dust in the air. Evening light settled like a coat of rust.

At the ranch house we shook hands, an unexpected spontaneous gesture initiated simultaneously. The car idled smoothly as our hands clasped. When I closed the door I saw

Norm move to switch the telephone back on, his face focusing, furrowing.

— ⁓

Once my vague leanings to leave had been voiced, my absorption in ranch work began slipping away. The wildlife and the land held my attention, but the unending maintenance of machinery, and the seasonal planting, irrigating, dawn-to-dusk push to produce lost its grip.

I had never managed to shed my outsider status. More accurately, I had never felt permanently moored; therefore, I felt poised to leave, both physically and emotionally. The house looked the same as the day I'd moved in. When I left, the collection of buildings would quickly regain their dry, decaying state of abandonment. Beyond Pete Hahn, the waitress at the cafe, the few men who stopped to buy hay, those neighbors I'd come to recognize enough to nod to when our trucks passed each other, no one would even notice my departure.

The novelty and challenge of ranch work had evaporated; the blizzard and dirt-filled winds had injected a sense of desperation and hopelessness into my experience with agricultural life. What hadn't waned was my attachment to and appreciation for the plains. The austere, unloved, enduring landscape had etched a deep impression, in contrast to the more superficial thrill of ranch living. When I considered Norman's suggestion to stay on, find a woman, accept a rural occupation, I could never visualize myself in the scenario.

One evening I overcame a surge of self-consciousness (what if a neighbor saw me?) and carried my sleeping bag down to the cottonwood haven at Little Horse Creek. I arrived in the still coolness of twilight, the time in a summer day that feels like a long relieved sigh. Bluebirds flew from fence posts in front of me.

Dozens of times I had climbed through the barbed wire, watched for the shadow of owls, stood still and surveyed for coyote and deer, walked through the dead crackling leaves beneath the rough-barked trees. I felt, even then, that I would remember the grove more precisely than the layout of the house I'd lived in over the year.

I sat on the gentle slope away from the creek while night came on like a slow deep tide. The owl returned to the nest, and I could hear the clamor of its young looking for food. The old unused windmill stood limned against the darkening sky.

I thought again about the couple. I imagined them when they'd first arrived, before disappointment and the bitterness of unrewarded labor hardened their postures. They were vigorous in their hope, keyed up by the risk they had taken, seeing potential in the contours of their land, standing together in the same evening light outside their home. Perhaps an owl would interrupt the silence, announcing the hunting time of day.

The fresh challenge, their new aspirations, the satisfaction of home-building and cultivating infused my imaginary settlers. At twilight, with the day's clamor behind them and the curve of plains surrounding them, the man and woman would stand outside their home without speaking. Each of them would let the busyness of the day settle like a wind dying out, the preoccupations of their separate concerns fade, until, in the chill, they moved together, leaned against each other, listened in silence to the rustling plains night come alive.

Those human phantoms had come to mean a great deal to me. It didn't matter whether the truth of the place had any connection to my fantasy. They had become companions during a time when I had had few real people to be with. All that year I had observed. Even as I participated I stood apart. At a different time of life I might have fit myself in more easily, circumstances might have brought me friendships, lovers. But I had chosen to stay alone, and had been let alone. My most significant human communion had been within my own thoughts.

A bright planet pierced the cloak of sky, a sky still tinged pink over the mountains. As night deepened, sounds took precedence over sights. The owls were active, their penetrating calls a warning to small lives. A coyote yapped in the distance, one bark, but no answering chorus. The stars brightened in intensity as I listened to the cautious movements of creatures comfortable in the darkness.

I woke many times during the night. My sleeping bag lay just under the owls' tree and usually, when I surfaced from sleep, the echo of their hooting rang in my ears. The stars turned slowly around Polaris. A hard silver half moon rode along its slow unvarying path. My sleep was light, too, because all night I sensed life and the ghosts of life moving decorously around me. Stirrings we shut ourselves away from in our hard box homes, as if we could arrogantly ignore the language of the earth.

The handshake with Norman, the night spent under the cottonwoods, the final images of settlers, those were the symbolic gestures of my transition. Without an imposed timetable or preconceived agenda, it had become time to leave. Arbitrarily, I set a date and gave my notice, relegating Norman to another summer of part-time help by doing so.

What had begun as a few days of interesting work, almost an impulsive lark, had evolved into a year-long immersion in a foreign and previously unappreciated corner of life. When I started, I didn't know enough to put diesel fuel into a tractor. I couldn't tell wheat from barley in a field. It had been like exploring an entirely new layer of existence, another plane of social interaction, a milieu of work and landscape and human dealings as divorced from the rest of my history as life in a ghetto.

By the end of it I had learned enough about rural work to avoid looking foolish most of the time. I had felt the relentless power of a tractor, knew the satisfaction to be had in looking over a wide, furrowed field of tender wheat shoots. I could spot a sick cow and had seen calves slither from womb into life. I had witnessed the panic in cows' eyes when they suddenly knew what lay in store.

The shy taciturnity of rural men had become a characteristic I valued. I understood their penchant for enforced loneliness, both the strength and desperation of their lives. I had been befriended by a man who believed no one could be worth eight dollars an hour, a man who had discovered the simple fulfillment of family and place and wanted nothing more. And another man who hung by his arms from rafters rather than get his back looked at by a doctor.

More profoundly, I had become intimate with the moods of an unheralded place. The plains environment imprinted itself on my psyche—patterns made of light and wind and aching space, tortured but enduring land, life where one expects none.

More than anything, I left with a mental file drawer jammed with plains impressions—coyotes barking through a light snow, a full moon astride the horizon, the howl of a hundred-mile gale with nothing in its path, the exultant pressure in my chest when I stood alone, a breathing silhouette on the wide, wide land.